SHOES

SHOES

A CELEBRATION OF PUMPS, SANDALS, SLIPPERS & MORE

By Linda O'Keeffe

Featuring photography by Andreas Bleckmann

WORKMAN PUBLISHING • NEW YORK

Library of Congress Cataloging-In-Publication Data
O'Keeffe, Linda
Shoes: A Celebration of Pumps, Sandals, Slippers & More   p. cm.

ISBN: 978-0-7611-0114-7
1. Shoes. I. Title.
GT2130.054   1996   96-20755   391'.413—dc20   CIP

Art Director: Paul Gamarello / Designer: Janet Vicario

Workman books are available at special discounts when purchased in bulk for premiums and sales promotions
as well as for fund-raising or educational use. Special editions or book excerpts can also be created to specification.
For details, contact the Special Sales Director at the address below, or send an email to specialmarkets@workman.com.

Workman Publishing Company Inc., 225 Varick Street, New York, NY 10014-4381

workman.com
WORKMAN is a registered trademark of Workman Publishing Co., Inc.
Manufactured in China
First printing October 1996

30 29 28 27 26 25 24 23

To Maggie Linehan
& James O'Keeffe

ACKNOWLEDGMENTS

Thanks to all the shoe designers whose limitless imaginations and craftsmanship made this book possible.

Ruth Sullivan, my editor, deserves special thanks. Her vision, guidance and tireless work brought this book to fruition. Thanks to Janet Vicario for her inspired design; to Joni Miller for her expertise, creative editing and writing; to Diane Botnick and Anita Dickhuth for their support and help; and to Andreas Bleckmann who painstakingly shot hundreds of shoes for the book—his expert photography shows off each shoe in its best light.

My gratitude to the following collectors who kindly let us photograph their shoes: Allan & Suzi, Sharlot Battin, Diane Blell, Ellen Carey, Deluxe Junk, Anne Fortescue, Henny Garfunkel, Cora Ginsberg Inc., Kim Hastreiter, Jane Starr Antiques, Katy K., Sandra Long, William Ivey Long, Barbara Melser-Lieberman, Anne Ogden, Carlo Pompeii, Angel Resnick, Sarajo, Azy Schecter, Schwarz & Benjamin, Screaming Mimi's, Joan Vass, Sara Vass and William Doyle Galleries.

I am indebted to the following for contributing their time, materials and information:

James Arpad, Barneys New York, Charles Bricker, Billy Cole, Stella Dallas, Frank De Caro, Joe Dolce, Anne Fegent, Robert Forest, Stephen Gray, Harry's Shoes, Dylan Landis, Michael Lassell, Cathy Laycock, Beth Levine, Harriet Lyons, Anne McDonnell, Sigerson Morrison, Cynthia Oliver, Andrea Rosen, Raimunda Salazar, Sterling Last Company, E. Vogel, Inc. and Donna Warner.

Warm appreciation to Melissa Evins and Reed Evins for generously sharing their vast collection and their knowledge of the shoe world; to Mary Trasko for extending her openhanded professionalism; and to Glenn Roberts for his valuable advice and for entrusting us with his remarkable Lotus shoe collection.

And thanks to the following institutions: Bally Shoe Museum, The Bata Shoe Museum, Bavarian National Museum, Charles Jourdan Museum, Cordwainers College, The Fashion Institute of Technology, *Footwear News,* French Footwear Manufacturers Association, Italian Trade Commission, The Metropolitan Museum of Art, Musée de la Chaussure, Museo Salvatore Ferragamo and Northampton Museums and Art Gallery.

CONTENTS

INTRODUCTION

A fresh start, a promise of romance and excitement—all little girls grow up believing the Cinderella myth that shoes can magically transform their lives. "Every woman has a conscious or subconscious desire to feel romantic," says shoe designer Stuart Weitzman.

Shoes are a force for change, a means of shedding the past and buying into the future. For much of history women's shoes were kept in the dark, concealed beneath a froth of petticoats or a ballooning crinoline. But while they were one of the most closeted parts of a woman's attire, ironically they were and are one of the most revealing. Eyes may be the windows to the soul, but shoes are the gateway to the psyche.

Psychologists have vigorously explored the hidden meaning of shoes from phallic symbols to secret vessels. Some say that the woman who collects shoes is a frustrated traveler; others suggest she is symbolically searching for

Susan Bennis
Warren Edwards, 1995

enlightenment. A pair of new shoes "might not cure a broken heart or soothe a tension headache," writes fashion critic Holly Brubach, "but they will relieve the symptoms and chase away the blues." Even the least vain among us has been known to blow an entire week's salary on an irresistible new pair.

Paul Mayer, 1984

In fact, the average American woman owns at least 30 pairs of shoes; the passionate collector owns in the hundreds. A woman with a standing order for each new variation of her favorite shoe style is simply putting into practice what every footwear fancier knows—when you find a shoe you love, buy it in every color. For if your body lets you down, your feet will still lift your spirits. "Feet don't gain or lose weight," observed Sara Vass, a collector who lives with more than 500 pairs of shoes. "You might not be able to wear your favorite pair of pants if you gain a few pounds, but you can always wear your favorite pairs of shoes." However, the charismatic qualities of shoes have more to do with possession than with use. It's the reason

French,
18th century

women continue buying shoes even though they wear only a
few of the many they own. It's why an adored shoe is rarely dis-
carded, even if it is unwearable.

Shoes have always reflected the wearer's status and
economic position. Aristocratic early 19th-century women
wore paper-thin slippers of brocade, their soles too fragile
to withstand even a few steps outdoors, while their
maids toiled in sturdy black leather boots. The gold-
soled sandals of Roman empresses, the red-heeled pumps of the court of
Louis XIV and the contemporary Gucci loafer have all served as calling
cards of class and wealth.

Shoes not only reflect social history, they are a personal
record of our lives—touchstones that evoke a time, a place, an emo-
tion. As mementos of occasions on which they were worn, shoes
preserve the past, triggering memories as vivid as those in a
photo album—the poignancy of a child's tiny first shoe immortalized

François Pinet, 1870

in bronze, the sweet sentiment of wedding slippers tucked away in their original box.

The indefinable allure of a new shoe unlocks rich private fantasies. We fall for a fabulous shoe at first glance, seduced by the tilt of a heel or the sensuous line of an arch. The whimsy of a flirtatious bow, the nearly edible appeal of a decorative frosting of beads or swirls of embroidery all add up to fatal attraction. The impulse to buy has nothing to do with need—it's the thrill of slipping into a new shoe and a new persona that piques desire. There may be reassurance in an old shoe, but no enchantment. Tedium comes with familiarity, and once a shoe is worn and comfortable, it loses its talismanic quality.

When it comes to shoes, practicality and comfort are beside the point. It may be one reason that 88 percent of all women buy shoes that are one

André Perugia, 1950s

Victorian wedding shoe

size too small for them. Shoes can be witty and drop-dead gorgeous, but not very comfortable. All too often they don't fit like a glove or conform to the foot's natural contours. But that really doesn't matter, admits clothing designer Diane von Furstenberg: "You look down at your feet and wink at yourself."

Manolo Blahnik, 1980s

And so, at the junction of fantasy and reality, women unhesitatingly choose frivolity over fit. While the idea of comfort is appealing—no one actually wants aching feet—in her heart a woman craves a sexy mule. Sensible shoes command respect, but high heels solicit adoration. A Birkenstock may offer deliverance, but a Blahnik promises adventure.

THE MAKING OF A SHOE

More than 100 operations go into the construction of a shoe. The first and most important step is the creation of the last, a hand-carved wood or molded plastic replica of the human foot. It alone determines the contour of the arch and how evenly the wearer's weight will be distributed throughout the foot, both of which are critical in establishing comfort.

A different last is required for each shoe style, whether the shoe is handmade or mass-

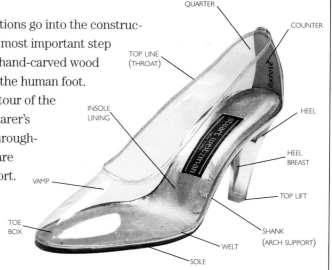

QUARTER

COUNTER

TOP LINE (THROAT)

INSOLE LINING

HEEL

HEEL BREAST

VAMP

TOP LIFT

TOE BOX

SHANK (ARCH SUPPORT)

WELT

SOLE

A last is carved, measured and refined to replicate the foot.

produced. Lastmaking demands great skill and a trained eye for fashion. After recording as many as 35 measurements from a "footprint" that shows the distribution of body weight, the maker judges the symmetry of the toes, calibrates the girth of the instep and ball of the foot, and calculates the height of the big toe and the contour of the instep. He also estimates how the foot will move inside the shoe.

The lastmaker's challenge is to address all these ratios without compromising the architectural beauty of the shoe design. For a heeled shoe, he visualizes the heel height, then proportionately determines the size of the throat. Next the appropriate height of the shoe's quarter is established: too high and it will rub the tendons; too low and the shoe will fail to grip the foot properly. Most crucial to the fit of a shoe is the measurement of the shank curve, the area that includes the ball and instep of the foot, because this is where the body's weight falls when the foot is in motion.

Then, using the last as a guide, the patternmaker cuts out the shoe's upper and lining, bevels the edges to ensure a good fit and sews the pieces together. Next he constructs a toe box, adds the counter (a stiffener for the shoe's back) and soaks the leather so it will easily conform to the lines of the last. A master craftsman carefully positions the upper on the last, tautly stretching it before nailing it tightly in place. The upper dries on the last for two weeks before the sole and heel can be attached.

In the final steps, finishers trim the welt, pare the heel, burnish the sole and add the insole lining. Last but not least, the shoe is polished and buffed—and ready to wear.

Nine lasts with fashionable toe shapes identified by year, style name and last number

I. THE SHOE MUST GO ON: THE SANDAL

Given their simple construction, it's not surprising that sandals were the first crafted footwear, the successors to primitive wrappings. Every ancient civilization seems to have had its own version of the basic design: a stiff sole fitted with straps or thongs. As early as 3500 B.C. the Egyptians made imprints of their feet in wet sand, molded braided papyrus into soles the same size and attached rawhide thongs to keep them on the foot. Eminently practical, these sandals were worn as protection from rough terrain and scorching sand, but they also left the foot almost completely uncovered and on display —a feature Egyptian women took advantage of by adorning them with jewels. The soles of sandals

Egyptian workers' sandals, 2000 B.C.

A 3,500-year-old palm sandal from Thebes. Preceding page: André Perugia, 1928.

worn by Roman empresses were made from poured gold; straps sparkled with encrustations of rare stones. The effect was dazzling and undeniably sexy.

The Japanese had braided sandals called zoris. Persians and Indians carved platform toe-knob sandals, and Africans sewed slip-on styles from colorfully pigmented leathers. Later the Slavs made sandals from felt; the Spanish, from rope. Even the British, despite their cold, wet climate, wore copies of sandals introduced by Mediterranean invaders. But all these versions were a far cry from their golden Egyptian ancestors.

Most shoes reveal something about the status of their wearer, but sandals have been alternately symbols of prestige or poverty, of chastity or coquetry. Plain wooden sandals were worn by the poor or humble in the Middle Ages; medieval priests

19th-century Indian toe-knob sandal, cast in the shape of a foot

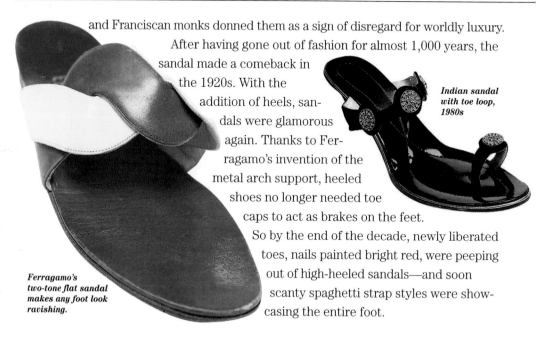

and Franciscan monks donned them as a sign of disregard for worldly luxury. After having gone out of fashion for almost 1,000 years, the sandal made a comeback in the 1920s. With the addition of heels, sandals were glamorous again. Thanks to Ferragamo's invention of the metal arch support, heeled shoes no longer needed toe caps to act as brakes on the feet.

So by the end of the decade, newly liberated toes, nails painted bright red, were peeping out of high-heeled sandals—and soon scanty spaghetti strap styles were showcasing the entire foot.

Indian sandal with toe loop, 1980s

Ferragamo's two-tone flat sandal makes any foot look ravishing.

Disco sandals, 1976

During the '60s, sandals became flat and earthy once again with the arrival of the sensibly orthopedic Birkenstock, but in the '70s they were pushed aside by high-heeled disco sandals made of vivid snakeskins and pearlized leathers. Fast and flashy, the disco style gave sandals a slightly tacky reputation. It took the finesse of designers such as Maud Frizon, Manolo Blahnik and Bennis Edwards in the '80s to legitimize high-heeled sandals by giving them the sophistication of closed-toe styles while preserving their sexiness. These designers showed us that the Egyptians were right after all: a well-designed sandal underscores the innate sensuality of the foot, giving its wearer the ability to flirt right down to her toes.

Manolo Blahnik chose saucy stripes and kid-lined suede for his peekaboo high-heeled sandal.

RAWHIDE SANDALS, worn by the Acholi people of Uganda, had extra-wide soles to protect the wearer's foot from hot or stony surfaces. The leather was decoratively scored and inlaid with natural pigments.

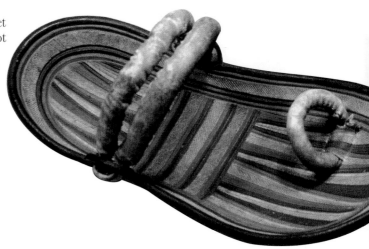

UGANDAN, 1890s

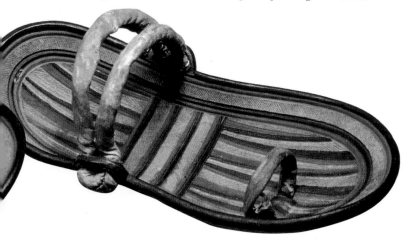

Hides used in African sandal-making were traditionally softened in cow dung, then cured between layers of mangrove bark.

SANDALS were made to order for torrid zones; their open tops allowed air to circulate freely. These ancient examples from diverse cultures are crafted from rawhide (near right), woven yucca fiber and wood (far right). The Egyptian sandals are missing their straps, which were probably of woven papyrus.

PERUVIAN, C. 6TH CENTURY

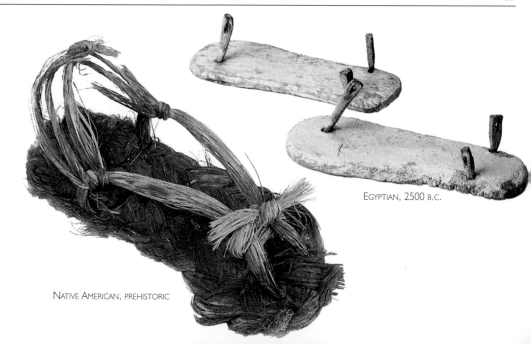

EGYPTIAN, 2500 B.C.

NATIVE AMERICAN, PREHISTORIC

THE CENTURIES-OLD toe knob originated in the Near East. In India, where Hindu belief forbids the use of cowhide, sandals are made of wood, which is sometimes sheathed with intricately worked silver.

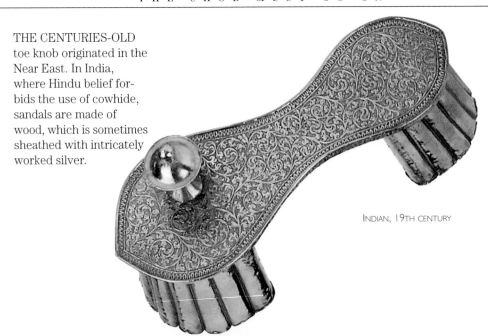

INDIAN, 19TH CENTURY

THE WESTERN version of the toe knob first popped up in the '60s, inspired by space-age technology. In Blahnik's sandal, a clear plastic instep band leaves the foot looking naked and focuses attention on the toes.

MANOLO BLAHNIK, 1992

A THREE-CORNERED style thong is a popular means of both securing and dressing up a sandal. The traditional Masai sandal has a squared-off toe and heel and rawhide thong; the American design is fashioned of ponyskin and gold metallic.

MASAI, 20TH CENTURY

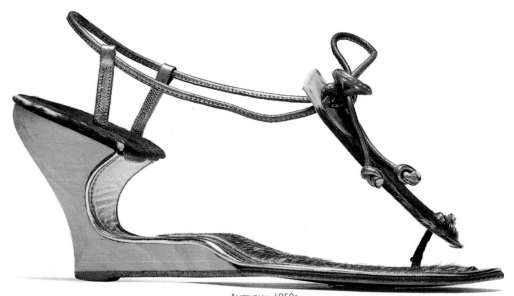

AMERICAN, 1950s

MOROCCAN-BORN Joseph Azagury is best known for simple, sensual sandals with flowing lines like this sling-back thong. Anne Klein refined the basic style with a rose between the toes. The soles of African flip-flop thongs (facing page) provide an ideal, if hidden, surface for decoration and/or advertising.

JOSEPH AZAGURY, 1990s

WEST AFRICAN, 1990S

ANNE KLEIN II,
1990S

Egyptians and Romans drew the faces of their enemies on the soles of their sandals so they could literally step on them.

WOODEN SANDALS
with toe and heel stilts
have been widely worn in
Asia and Africa. This pair
attached to the foot by
means of a leather toe
thong and vamp strap.

PAKISTANI/AFGHAN, 19TH CENTURY

PAKISTANI, 20TH CENTURY

COLORFUL *CHAPPALS*, worn in the hot and sandy Indus valley, are designed to be functional: the pom-poms protect the toes and the narrow open backs enable the wearer to easily rid the shoes of sand.

A CUFF-LIKE STRAP over the instep dominates the design of this suede slide. The giant stud-like decorations are repeated around the front of the sole, making the slide look a bit like a tugboat.

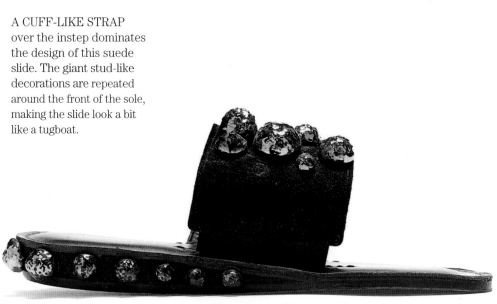

STEVEN ARPAD, 1950s

IVORY MOSAIC INLAY
adorns the soles of these
wooden sandals used
by Syrian women at the
public baths.

SYRIAN, 1900

A DRESS SANDAL from the Bolivian highlands is an eclectic blend of two cultures. The ancient sandal shape and silver condor buckle are of native Indian origin, while the fashionable heel and platform sole are Spanish.

BOLIVIAN, EARLY 20TH CENTURY

SILVER KID and black suede dress up this evening dance shoe. Its sturdy sole allowed for a full night of dancing while its open toes kept the foot cool.

BALLY, 1934

THE LOOK OF METAL
against bare skin has
always been considered
erotic. Weitzman hung
a string of gold charms on
the upper of this cork
thong, while Azagury
embellished his "Roman"
sandal (facing page) with
golden chains.

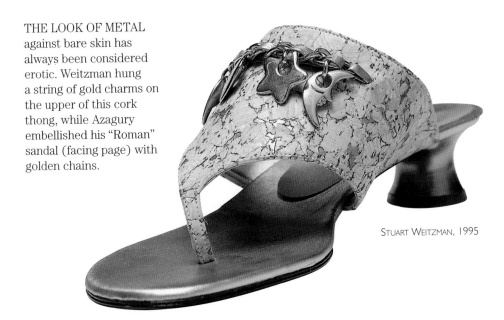

STUART WEITZMAN, 1995

Aphrodite, the Greek goddess of love, was often depicted naked except for a pair of sandals.

JOSEPH AZAGURY, 1990s

DAVID EVINS, shoemaker to the stars, helped restore glamorous, ultra-feminine footwear to the stage and screen of the '50s. He designed these pearl-encrusted satin sandals for Lena Horne.

DAVID EVINS, 1962

HALSTON, 1980s

AMERICAN, 1950s

CELEBRITY SHOES not only spawn fads in the fashion world but are sometimes assigned almost holy-relic status by fans. The strappy evening sandals above were fashioned for Elizabeth Taylor. At left are the ornate wedge sandals worn by Lana Turner for her role in the 1955 film *The Prodigal*.

Before there was Manolo Blahnik or Robert Clergerie, there was André Perugia, the first of the "celebrity" shoe designers. Born in Nice in 1893 to a shoemaker father, Perugia lost no time in proving himself a prodigy. He opened a shop at age 16 and quickly made a name for himself, introducing new heel and vamp shapes that eventually far surpassed his father's workaday styles in their artistry, their daring and their price. As far as Perugia was concerned, however, money was never the issue. "The wealthiest woman in the world couldn't pay me to make her an ugly pair of shoes," he was known to say.

Cubist sandal, 1930

Sensuous figure-eight straps caress the foot on this suede sandal, 1920s.

It was this pursuit of beauty that Perugia made his lifelong ambition, fashioning customized pumps and sandals from jewel-toned snakeskin, purple suede, gold kid and pearlized lizard. Society women who flocked to the French Riviera for the winter season were dazzled by his work and by Perugia himself—a handsome, dapper man with an Old World charm. But it was through his association with the world-famous couturier Paul Poiret that his success was assured. At the end of World War I, he hired the

Perugia hunts for the perfect size among his 100,000 lasts, 1951.

Prototype for a marcasite chain sandal

Evening pump for Rita Hayworth, 1950

young Perugia to design for him. And Perugia, who now had a shop on Paris' Faubourg St. Honoré, agreed.

Among his clients were stars of the Folies Bergère and movie actresses who wanted shoes that epitomized the glamour of the stage. Perugia did not disappoint them. He transformed Josephine Baker's trademark turban into a quilted kidskin sandal, and he fashioned black lace heels for movie siren Gloria Swanson. His commissioned shoes began to acquire the character of three-dimensional portraits.

Always eager to experiment with new materials, shapes and textures, Perugia continued to create shoes of startling originality throughout a 50-year association with I. Miller and

Perfectly poised stiletto sandal, 1950s

Prow-toe sandal, 1960   *"Turban" sandal, 1928*   *"Mask" sandal, 1929*

then with Charles Jourdan. And since he was known to talk to his shoes, he earned a reputation as an eccentric as well as a genius. In his book *From Eve to Rita Hayworth*, a collection of psychological portraits, Perugia theorized that the way to unveil a woman's personality was to study her feet. Of course, if those feet were shod in a pair of Perugia sandals, the observer would have to conclude that here was a woman who loved drop-dead glamour at all costs.

WARTIME RATIONING
and a limit on imports
resulted in Ferragamo's
innovative use of materi-
als. Here kidskin cord is
teamed with packing
string for a surprisingly
sophisticated look.

SALVATORE FERRAGAMO, 1938

A WITTY STRAW sandal from Ferragamo makes use of raffia, perhaps inspired by beach hats, and four corks to form the heel.

SALVATORE FERRAGAMO, 1935

THE THONG is the string
bikini of the shoe world.
Levine (facing page) and
Giallombardo designed
sandals to leave the foot
looking as temptingly
naked as possible.

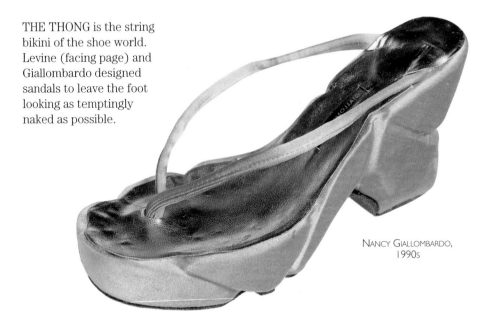

NANCY GIALLOMBARDO,
1990s

Throughout the 1930s and '40s, daytime shoes that revealed the toes were considered immodest.

BETH AND HERBERT LEVINE,
1960s

DIEGO DELLA VALLE, 1996

DELMAN'S '90s VERSION of the vamp sandal has the same high-closing ankle strap as its flapper cousin. Della Valle's spring line of sherbety sandals (facing page) puts the emphasis on the toe.

DELMAN, 1990s

THE "DEAUVILLE,"
Pfister's open basket-
weave plastic sandal, has
been copied more than
any other shoe in the
world.

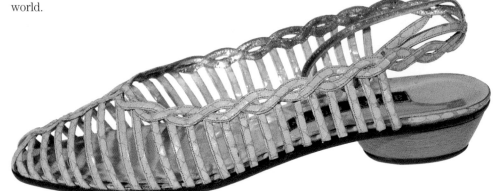

ANDREA PFISTER, 1979

1988

ANDREA PFISTER, 1974

TWO MULES from Pfister—the "Coquelicot" (above) with its flower corsage and the color-blocked "Homage to Mondrian" (left)—illustrate his penchant for elegant, sexy shoes.

FIAMMA FERRAGAMO follows in her father Salvatore's footsteps. As head of shoe production for the family company in Florence, she designs sandals that are fashionable, ultra-feminine yet comfortable.

FERRAGAMO, 1990s

FERRAGAMO invented the wedge heel in 1936, then used it on shoe styles from sandals to pumps and ankle boots over the next decade.

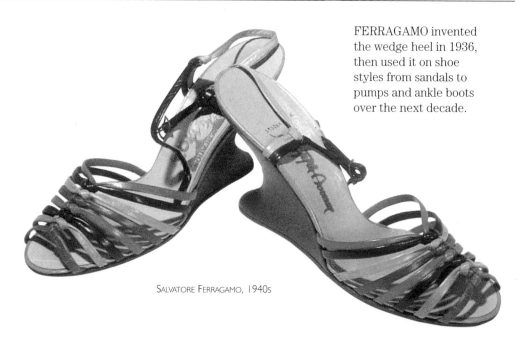

SALVATORE FERRAGAMO, 1940s

A MULTICOLORED pavé wedge sandal with tubular straps was part of the costume Evins fashioned for Claudette Colbert's screen Cleopatra. A decade later, he modified the design, making it practical for streetwear.

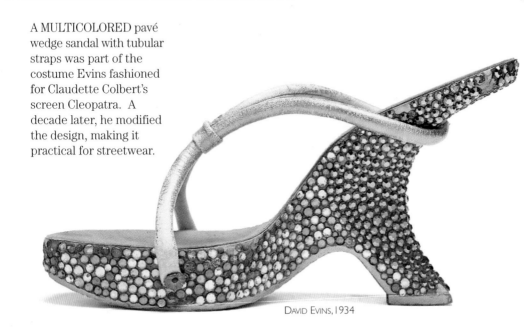

DAVID EVINS, 1934

DÉCOLLETÉ SANDALS with high heels were a fad in the '50s. Vivier's pavé version is rendered respectable by a wide ankle strap.

ROGER VIVIER, 1950s

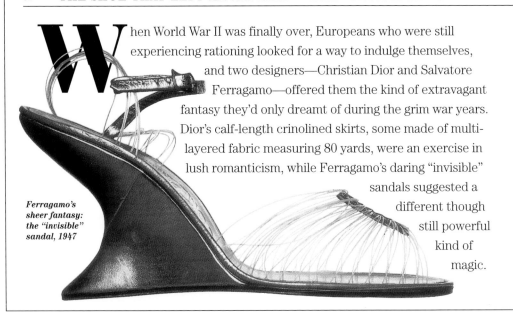

When World War II was finally over, Europeans who were still experiencing rationing looked for a way to indulge themselves, and two designers—Christian Dior and Salvatore Ferragamo—offered them the kind of extravagant fantasy they'd only dreamt of during the grim war years. Dior's calf-length crinolined skirts, some made of multi-layered fabric measuring 80 yards, were an exercise in lush romanticism, while Ferragamo's daring "invisible" sandals suggested a different though still powerful kind of magic.

Ferragamo's sheer fantasy: the "invisible" sandal, 1947

During the war years, leather had been used exclusively for soldiers' boots, so shoemakers were forced to make sandal uppers from felt, hemp, straw and textiles. Many were frustrated, but Ferragamo saw this restriction as a creative challenge and pioneered the use of materials such as cellulose and paper of the sort used for candy wrappers, which he would braid with gold threads into delicate sandal straps. One day, after the war had ended, it occurred to him as he watched fishermen on the Arno river in Florence that nylon fishing line might be used to make a transparent vamp.

Ferragamo's "invisible" sandal with high heel, 1947

To create the illusion of an invisible shoe, he first tunneled into a wooden wedge heel and extracted the interior so that the foot would appear to float when mounted on top of it. He then formed a vamp by passing strands of nylon from one side to the other through holes in the insole.

Influenced by Cubist art, Ferragamo's illusion made use of the idea of shifting perspectives. In certain lights, the vamp seemed to disappear, while from certain angles the heel seemed to be suspended in midair. Yet despite such artistry and an avalanche of publicity, the sandals hardly sold. The designer believed it was because women felt too exposed in them, though some argued that it was the price that was offputting. Why buy

A '90s knockoff of Ferragamo's see-through vamp

Nina, 1960s

a pair of "invisible" shoes for $29.75, asked a *Look* magazine article, when you could buy four tons of coal for the same price?

But perhaps his ingenious fantasy was simply too visionary and too deconstructed for postwar women yearning for excess and decoration. Ironically, one of Beth Levine's experiments in invisibility, the topless high heel of the 1960s, also met with lukewarm public response. But a less refined variation of the invisible sandal was popular in the 1960s. The style was not so much futuristic as Las Vegas showgirl, with the heels or throats of high-heeled versions flashily outlined with a strip of rhinestones. Although the shoes themselves were nearly invisible, they revealed all. Of course, a perfectly formed foot and a good pedicure were essential to the look.

Neiman Marcus, 1960s

A RIBBON CANDY
confection, Beth Levine's
graceful, undulating
version of the invisible
sandal exhibits an
unusually animated use
of acrylic.

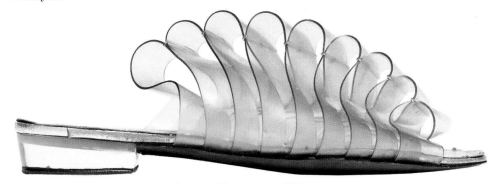

BETH AND HERBERT LEVINE, 1950s

THE PLASTIC JELLY, originally molded to look like a French fisherman's sandal, has been worn by toddlers for decades. In the '90s, Cox reintroduced it in the form of cheeky streetwear for grown-ups.

PATRICK COX, 1993

CHARLES JOURDAN, best known for his understated, no-nonsense shoes, reveals a playful streak in this see-through sandal with a cluster of cherries on top.

CHARLES JOURDAN, 1980s

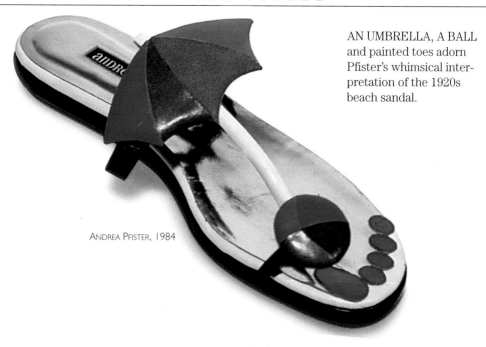

AN UMBRELLA, A BALL and painted toes adorn Pfister's whimsical interpretation of the 1920s beach sandal.

ANDREA PFISTER, 1984

SILK FLOWERS TURN
a pair of sandals into a
spring bonnet. The open
back and strappy ankle
ties are almost comically
sexy.

BERNARD FIGUEROA,
1994

igh heels are a paradox," wrote Rona Berg in *Vogue*. "They can make a woman appear more—or less—powerful." When worn over long periods of time, they are a devilish prescription for pain, responsible for everything from hammertoes to fallen arches. But when worn for effect, like Cinderella's glass slippers, they can work magic and bestow the power to seduce.

Women may "wear" slippers, "put on" sneakers and "slip into" loafers, but they "dress" in high heels. They playact. Psychologically, high heels permit them to lead rather than follow. An ordinary woman becomes a towering seductress, literally staring men down. Sexually, whether she acknowledges it or not, she can choose to become the subject or the object of male worship.

The shoe lover's eternal dilemma: the perfect pump in the wrong size. Preceding page: Jan Jansen, 1996.

Physically, it is impossible for a woman to cower in high heels. She is forced to take a stand, to strike a pose, because anatomically her center of gravity has been displaced forward. Her lower back arches, her spine and legs seem to lengthen and her chest thrusts forward. Her calves and ankles appear shapelier, and her arches seem to heave out of her shoes.

Dries Van Noten, 1995

Design critic Stephen Bayley referred to the effect as one of "twanging sinew, of tension needing to be released." High heels force a woman's foot into the vertical posture described by sex researcher Alfred Kinsey as typical during female sexual arousal, when "the whole foot may be extended until it falls in line with the rest of the leg."

The history of heels is murky, although they surely date back to pre-Christian times. Egyptian butchers wore heels to raise their feet above the carnage, and Mongolian horsemen had their boots heeled to grip their stirrups more firmly. But the first recorded year that

Steven Arpad, 1950s

heels were worn for reasons of vanity was 1533, when the diminutive Catherine de Médicis brought heels from Florence to Paris for her upcoming marriage to the Duke d'Orléans. The style was immediately adopted by ladies of the French court.

In the next century, European women tottered on heels 5 inches and higher, balancing themselves with canes so as not to fall on their faces. Because the working class couldn't afford to wear such impractical shoes, heels became a sign of privilege. Not surprisingly, with the toppling of the French

Charles Hind's 5-inch wooden heel with kidskin, 1890

monarchy, shoe heights fell, too. And thereafter they rose or fell according to the whims of fashion and the dictates of politics and social etiquette.

In the mid 19th century, following a rage for basic, flat slippers, the heeled shoe once again became the predominant style. Although Europe pioneered the new trend for high heels, America wasn't far behind in adopting the style. In 1888 the first heel factory in the United States opened, making it unnecessary for fashion-conscious women to import their shoes from Paris.

Newly liberated, women in the early part of the 20th century favored sturdy, sensible shoes. But in the 1920s, as hemlines rose, legs and feet were suddenly on display and shoes needed to be as beautiful as they were practical. Glittering shoes—high-heeled and strappy—epitomized the free-wheeling hedonism of the era.

Always teetering in and out of style, heels reached new heights with the advent of the stiletto in the 1950s. And to the dismay of many women, spindly high heels popped up again in fashion magazines in the 1990s. Still, whether a woman thinks heels are the height of fashion or the height of absurdity, she usually has at least one pair in the back of her closet for the occasion when sensible shoes just won't do.

Bernard Figueroa,
1995

ROGER VIVIER, 1960

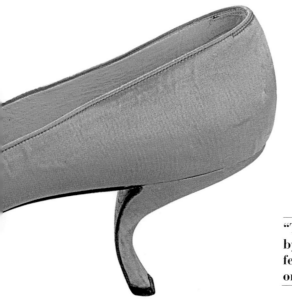

ROGER VIVIER, known for his innovative heel shapes and delicious ornamentation, designed this bejeweled pair with "comma" heels.

"To be carried by shoes, winged by them. To wear dreams on one's feet is to begin to give reality to one's dreams." *—Roger Vivier*

THIS RED HEEL,
its vamp and tongue
encrusted with silver
lace appliqué, heralds
the regal ostentation
of Rococo style.

PORTUGUESE, C. 1695

ALSATIAN, C. 1700

A THICK, CURVED heel
and needle-nose toe
characterized the shoe
silhouette of the early
1700s. An artistic use of
punchwork on the upper
results in striking patterns.

*Red heels, a
status symbol in
17th- and 18th-century
Europe, were worn only
by the privileged classes.*

CLOG-LIKE OVERSHOES called pattens were strapped onto fine, fragile shoes to protect them from muddy European streets. Matching shoe-and-patten sets were popular in the 18th century.

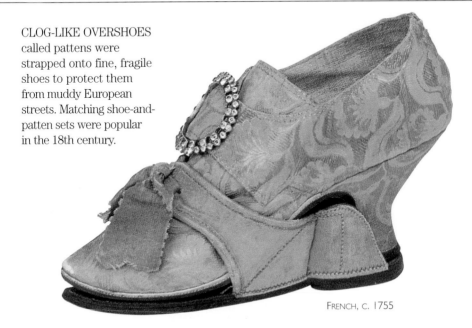

FRENCH, c. 1755

A WAISTED HEEL set off the latticework on this silk-satin latchet shoe, whose instep flaps criss-crossed into a jeweled buckle.

FRENCH, C. 1760

A WIDE, STURDY HEEL was preferred by the English gentry, in contrast to the more delicate style favored by their Continental counterparts. Over time, the English would turn their sensibly shod image into a world reputation for fine custom-made footwear.

ENGLISH, 1730s

The "Louis" heel, splayed at the base and waisted, originated at the French court of Louis XV and has been used by designers to this day.

ENGLISH, 1730s

POSITIONED under the arch, the heels of these French pumps lent support but caused the front of the foot to be crushed in the upturned toe, forcing women to teeter awkwardly.

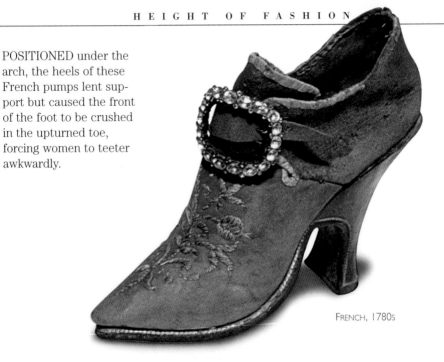

FRENCH, 1780s

French, 1780s

French, 1730s

"Mount on French heels
when you go to a ball—
'Tis the fashion to totter
and show you can fall."
—*18th-century
satirical poem*

AFTER THE CRASH on Wall Street in 1929, frivolity was shelved in favor of austere practicality. This high-heeled court shoe for evening, however, was cut from luxurious gold kidskin.

O'CONNOR & GOLDBERG, 1930s

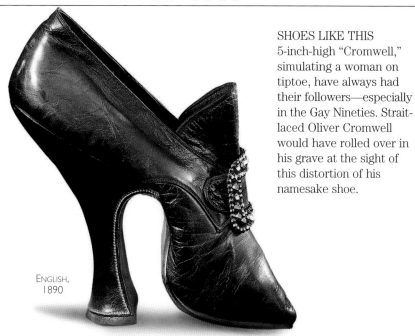

ENGLISH,
1890

SHOES LIKE THIS
5-inch-high "Cromwell,"
simulating a woman on
tiptoe, have always had
their followers—especially
in the Gay Nineties. Strait-
laced Oliver Cromwell
would have rolled over in
his grave at the sight of
this distortion of his
namesake shoe.

"Not diamonds but heels are a girl's best friend."   —*William Rossi*

STUART WEITZMAN,
1992

STUART WEITZMAN,
1994

PAUL MAYER,
1984

PAUL MAYER,
1984

PLAYING DECORATIVE games with heels, shoemakers have pushed their designs to the limit. Here, a sparkling array includes a hand-carved heel embedded with semiprecious nuggets, a pavé "cigarette" heel and a heel faceted like a gemstone. In the 18th century, similar creations were known as *venez-y-voir,* or "come hither," shoes.

TODD OLDHAM,
1994

AMERICAN,
1930s

LOUBOUTIN DREW on the curves of a woman's body for this sensuous heel. Rankins' inspiration for the heel on his "Marilyn" mule (facing page) was a table leg.

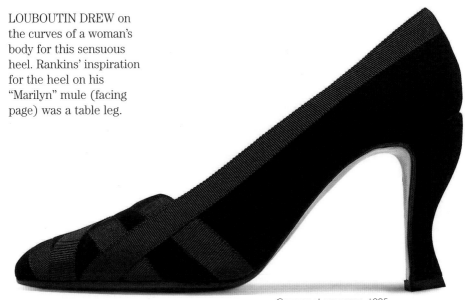

CHRISTIAN LOUBOUTIN, 1995

"If you rebel against high heels, take care to do so in a very smart hat."
—*George Bernard Shaw*

SCOTT RANKINS, 1993

In the 1960s, an adjustable-height "telescopic" shoe heel was patented in Oak Hill, Illinois.

ALBANESE OF ROME created this rooster mule with a geometric stacked heel at the same time that his company was pioneering the stiletto.

ALBANESE OF ROME, 1950s

IN THE ROARING '20S, a time of prohibition and political repression, women's footwear— such as this evening shoe of crimson velvet and gold calf—was at its most frivolous.

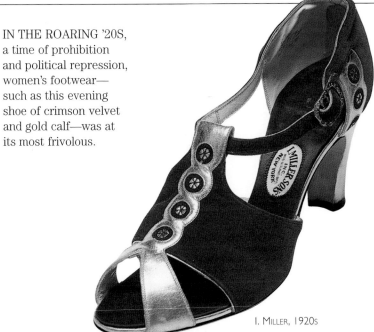

I. MILLER, 1920S

AN EYE-CATCHING HEEL
never takes a back seat,
whether it's Bakelite pin-
pointed with rhinestones
(near left) or velvet
with gold kid
overlay.

AMERICAN, 1950s

BALLY, 1930s

VIVIER EXECUTED his first heel inspired by a thorn in the early '60s. Moore exaggerated the cruel shape to fashion a fetish shoe.

Roger Vivier, 1990s

John Moore, 1980s

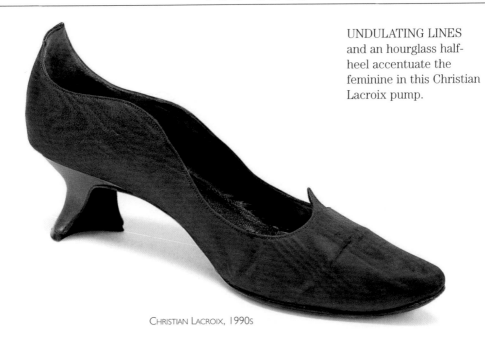

UNDULATING LINES
and an hourglass half-
heel accentuate the
feminine in this Christian
Lacroix pump.

CHRISTIAN LACROIX, 1990S

CHRISTIAN LOUBOUTIN, ALL 1990S

ROGER VIVIER, 1967

EVEN LOWER HEELS reflect Vivier's urge to embellish, as seen in this global version of the rhinestone ball heel that he designed for Marlene Dietrich in the '50s. Louboutin embedded real hydrangea petals in a Perspex heel (far left) and painted carved heels gold.

VIVIER'S BEADED evening pump is as fine-tuned as a delicate time-piece. By forcing the heel under the arch, elongating the vamp and turning up the toe, the designer achieved a shoe of perfectly balanced proportions.

ROGER VIVIER, 1967

> "Shoes, like buildings, have a mysterious chemistry of proportion."
> —*Suzanne Slesin*

Roger Vivier is the Fabergé of footwear. For six decades he has been creating designs that have gloriously redefined our notions of the shoe. Lighthearted and decorative, his shoes have all the charm of 18th-century styles but are very much of our time— their construction based on modern principles of aeronautics and engineering.

Vivier studied sculpture at the École des Beaux-Arts in Paris, and his designs show a sculptor's preoccupation with form and texture. In 1937 he opened his own atelier and began ghosting lines for top international firms such as I. Miller, Delman, Bally and Rayne. He joined the house of Dior in 1953, and his 10-year collaboration with the great couturier marked a golden era in shoe fashion.

The most visually arresting part of a Vivier shoe is often an innovative heel, named for the shape it mimics: the comma, spool, ball, needle, pyramid or escargot. For Marlene Dietrich, Vivier created a narrow high heel whose tip pierced a rhinestone pavé ball. His "comma" heels are still cast by an aeronautical

Paper maquette for a 1938 court shoe

Facing page: Roger Vivier at his 1987 Palais du Louvre retrospective.
Right: a 1990s version of his ball heel.

engineering firm in an ultralight aluminum alloy developed for jet engines.

Line is what makes Vivier's shoes live and it's what he fashions first, using paper maquettes as models. The fancy comes later, and it's not unusual for a heel to be embellished with a bunch of kingfisher plumes or embroidered with pearls.

For one of his more notable commissions, Vivier studded gold kidskin with

Vivier's heel innovations:

| *The "Comma"* | *The "Choc"* | *The "Needle"* |

garnets for the heels Queen Elizabeth wore to her coronation in 1953. Over the years he has customized footwear for such legendary celebrities as Josephine Baker, Jeanne Moreau, Catherine Deneuve and the Beatles.

"My shoes are sculptures," says Vivier of his creations, which are displayed in museums around the world. "They are quintessentially French, a Parisian alchemy in style."

| *A modified "Louis"* | *The "Prism"* | *The "Pyramid"* |

CONCAVE OR CONVEX, Vivier's heel shapes have had widespread influence. The inwardly bent heel of Demeulemeester's funky loafer looks like a fattened version of Vivier's *talon choc*. With his grosgrain pump (facing page), Mayer pays open tribute to Vivier's "comma" heel.

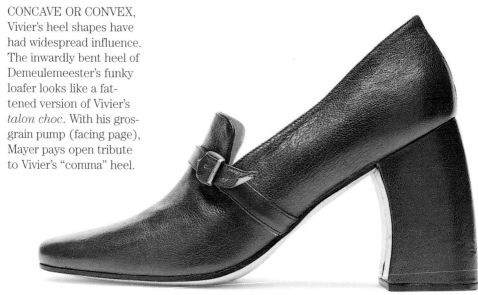

ANN DEMEULEMEESTER, 1995

"Put on your red shoes and dance the blues."—*David Bowie*

PAUL MAYER, 1991

THE ARCHITECTURE
of the heel is the corner-
stone of Figueroa's
aesthetic. These metal
spike heels were modeled
after tree branches, then
sculpted by hand.

BERNARD FIGUEROA, 1993

"There is so much space between a woman's heel and the floor that one can use." —*Bernard Figueroa*

BERNARD FIGUEROA, 1993

THROUGHOUT THE '50s, the heel of the foot was considered particularly erotic. Mules were all the rage, and attention was drawn to the naked heel by novel designs —from a porcelain China cameo to crystal disks and a coil of rhinestones.

SIR EDWARD RAYNE,
LATE 1950S

At the court of Louis XIV, men wore shoes whose heels were painted
with miniature rustic or romantic scenes.

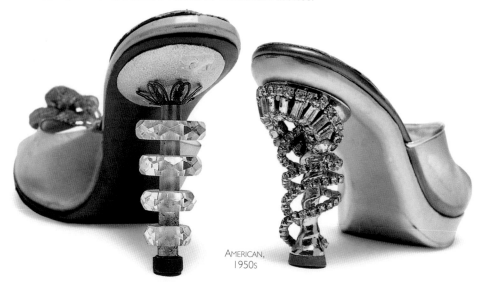

American,
1950s

"THIS SEASON'S PUMP," wrote British *Vogue* in 1959, "shows the long, lean grace of a wolf-hound . . . its height is the result of a sometimes skinny, sometimes waisted heel."

TAJ TAJERIE,
1959

THE TECHNOLOGICAL wizardry of Perugia's corkscrew heel may have stemmed from his stint as an engineer in a plane factory during World War I.

ANDRÉ PERUGIA, 1952

BETH LEVINE'S KIDSKIN
heel resembles a tightly
wound spool of silver
(below), while Steven
Arpad's "Ramshorn"
prototype heel is a nod
to classical Greek archi-
tecture (facing page).

BETH & HERBERT LEVINE, 1954

STEVEN ARPAD, 1930s

ALBANESE OF ROME, 1980s

FUNNEL-SHAPED heels, here resembling inverted pyramids, were a popular alternative to platforms during the late 1970s and early '80s.

FONTENAU, 1980s

THE STACKED BALL heel and starred upper on Pfister's "Trapèze Brodé" re-creates the circus-like whimsy of Holmes' striped patent-leather stiletto (facing page), even though the two were designed decades apart.

ANDREA PFISTER, 1994

"If you look under the table at any dinner party, most women will have kicked their shoes off."
—*Diego Della Valle*

HOLMES, 1957

O f all the miracles of modern shoe technology, the stiletto may stand as the greatest. Known as the needle, hatpin, flute, rapier and spike, the stiletto heel—all 4 inches of it—arrived on the fashion scene in 1952 on a classic pump with a pointed toe. It's not clear who came up with the idea: Ferragamo, Albanese of Rome and Dal Có produced "needle

Salvatore Ferragamo, 1950s

heels" around 1953 in Italy, about the same time that Roger Vivier created his version in Paris. The construction in each was the same and was not unlike that of a skyscraper, requiring

Roger Vivier, 1980

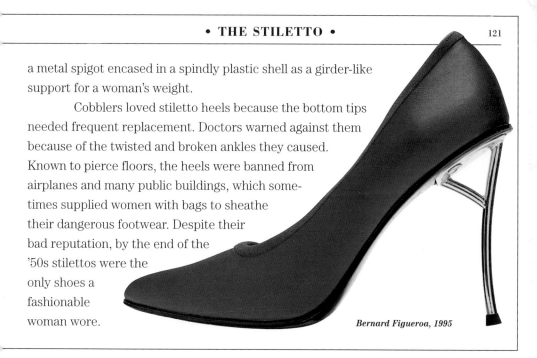

a metal spigot encased in a spindly plastic shell as a girder-like support for a woman's weight.

Cobblers loved stiletto heels because the bottom tips needed frequent replacement. Doctors warned against them because of the twisted and broken ankles they caused. Known to pierce floors, the heels were banned from airplanes and many public buildings, which some-times supplied women with bags to sheathe their dangerous footwear. Despite their bad reputation, by the end of the '50s stilettos were the only shoes a fashionable woman wore.

Bernard Figueroa, 1995

Seen as symbols of aggression, heightened sexuality and playful defiance, stiletto heels became the trademark of the naughty girl. Hollywood's Jayne Mansfield, who played the part to the hilt, owned 200 pairs.

By the 1960s, the popularity of the stiletto had waned as low-heeled boots and flats became the fashionable choice to wear with pantsuits and miniskirts. But the style reemerged in the late

Sexy arch revealers by Maud Frizon, 1985 (left) and Manolo Blahnik, 1995 (above)

'70s and still has its fans today, from fetishists and Madonna to a cartoon super-heroine in the TV show *The Tick*, who uses her stiletto as a lethal weapon to subdue her enemies.

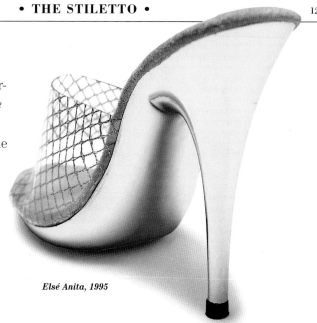

Elsé Anita, 1995

ELSÉ ANITA,
BOTH 1995

"How tall am I? Honey, with hair, heels and attitude I'm through this damned roof."
—*RuPaul*

PAUL MAYER, 1983

FERRULE HEELS
reached their height
in the 1970s and again
in the retro '90s. These
4½- and 5-inch heels both
sport snakeskin uppers
and ankle straps.

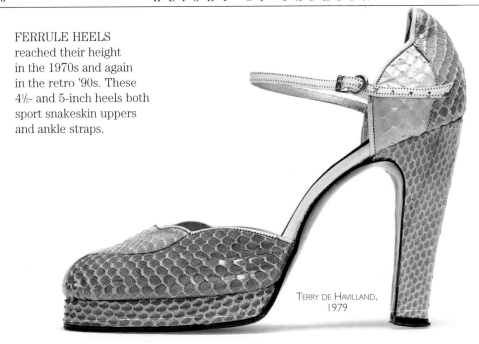

TERRY DE HAVILLAND,
1979

 According to Harper's Index, *the average increase in the protrusion of a woman's buttocks when she wears high heels is 25 percent.*

MICHEL PERRY, 1995

FOR A SNOW DOME effect, Patrick Cox encased a miniature Eiffel Tower in the plastic heel of his jelly.

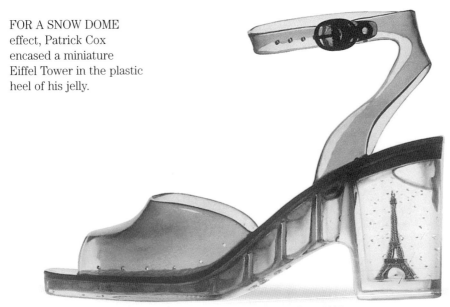

PATRICK COX, 1996

NADING, who designed this snub-nosed ankle-strap pump while still a student at New York City's Fashion Institute of Technology, carved its heel from a rod of Lucite.

LISA NADING, 1995

FRENCH DESIGNER
Cyd Jouny imagined
"a Texan princess on
holiday on the Côte
d'Azur" when she
designed this cross
between a basketball
sneaker and stiletto
mule.

CYD JOUNY, 1995

III. FEATS OF FANCY: SLIPPERS

Unfettered by functionality, slippers were designed not to be used but to be looked at. In fact, the word *slipper* defined any elegant, thin-soled shoe made of fabric or fine leather that barely covered the foot and slipped on and off with ease. Throughout history, slippers have been variously associated with wealth, prestige and—because they were so delicate and most often worn in the boudoir— intimacy. Roman women never appeared outdoors in their *socci,* so these flexible, low-heeled slip-ons took on erotic connotations. Senator Lucius Vitellius was even known to have concealed his lover's slipper beneath his tunic, discreetly

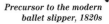

Precursor to the modern ballet slipper, 1820s

Bold stockings and fine silk slippers were usually obscured from view under voluminous Victorian skirts. Preceding page: Karl Lagerfeld, 1992.

removing it from time to time to kiss it rapturously as if it were a perfumed love letter.

Flat-soled slippers of brocaded silk or velvet had long been worn by the church's episcopal hierarchy, and by the time Elizabeth I took the throne, slippers with heels were the height of fashion in England for both men and women. Fabulously decorated and often made of precious materials, they were intended to signify the wearer's wealth. Indeed, in Venice, shoemakers added such an excessive amount of gold and gemstones to their creations that sumptuary laws were passed to limit their use. Nonetheless, slippers—the flimsier, the better—continued to be a sign of social standing. When Empress Josephine (who by one count owned 521 pairs) showed her shoemaker a slipper that had developed a hole after just one wearing, he is said to have responded: "Ah, madame, I see what the problem is. You have *walked* in them."

J. Sparkes Hall's slipper with machine stitching, 1855

Eighteenth-century jewel-encrusted slippers featured upturned toes, and middle-class women copied their social betters by wearing trompe l'oeil clogs decorated to look as if they were made of brocade, lace, ribbon and precious stones. Even after the French Revolution, when the red heels of the aristocracy were banned, delicate *escarpins* made of soft kid, velvet, silk and satin remained in vogue for nearly half a century.

In the 19th century, when balls became popular, slim slippers of tissue-thin kid or luxurious dress silk decorated with rosettes, pom-poms or bows were often danced threadbare. Because sensible shoes bore a working-class stigma, both European and American women of the middle and upper classes wore their impractical slippers outdoors, where even a few blades of grass would do irreparable harm. In 1832, in the

Aubusson embroidered slipper, 1820

midst of winter, it was not uncommon, wrote Mrs. Anthony Trollope, to see women hobbling over ice and snow "with their poor little toes pinched into a miniature slipper, incapable of excluding as much moisture as might bedew a primrose."

Today slippers are still purchased for special

*Turkish mule,
c. 1900*

occasions—to match an evening gown or wedding dress. And like many of those in Marie Antoinette's famous wardrobe of precious slippers, they are worn only once. Whether worn to a gala or only in the boudoir, however, modern slippers are often made from the same rich fabrics and decorated with the same kinds of embroidery, sequins and feathers as those of centuries ago. And true to form, their function is subservient to their sumptuous style.

*Nancy Giallombardo's
opulently beaded mule, 1995*

FLAT-SOLED SLIPPERS, though comfortable, tend to make the foot look wider. These "sandal slippers," secured with long silk ribbons, were fashioned with narrow soles for a slimmer look.

FRENCH, 1815

In the early 19th century, the term "slipper" was used to describe all delicate footwear.

A SILK COURT SHOE
with eyelet trim and
a rosette bow (below)
and roller-printed
patterns on leather
(facing page) typify the
broad spectrum of slipper
decoration.

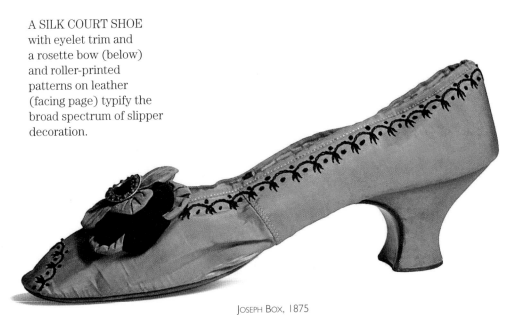

JOSEPH BOX, 1875

ENGLISH, C. 1800

Marie Antoinette employed a servant solely to tend to her 500 pairs of slippers, which were catalogued by date, color and style.

ITALIAN, C. 1860

FRENCH, C. 1855

FABRICS AND TRIMS have always challenged a shoemaker's imagination. These house slippers were probably constructed of hatmakers' straw. The vamps on "chameleon" slippers (facing page)—so called because they were available in many colors— peeped out beneath the cage-crinolined skirts of the mid 19th century.

BRIDES BEGAN wearing white slippers with their gowns in the mid 19th century—a tradition still observed today. Peter Fox's fantasy-filled line of wedding shoes (facing page) is ultra-feminine, with narrowed heel and toe.

AMERICAN AND ENGLISH,
C. 1870

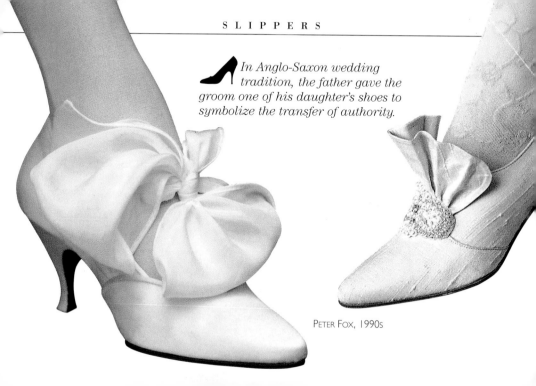

In Anglo-Saxon wedding tradition, the father gave the groom one of his daughter's shoes to symbolize the transfer of authority.

PETER FOX, 1990s

HELLSTERN & SONS,
c. 1905

WHETHER SILK or satin, no fabric was too delicate or expensive for a lady's slipper. The Hellstern label was synonymous with turn-of-the-century luxury. Maykopf's design was embroidered in point de chainette to match a shot-satin evening dress.

C. MAYKOPF, 1890s

ORNAMENTATION helped to preserve the vamp of a slipper as its body disintegrated from wear. In the 18th and 19th centuries, slippers often carried a line beneath the maker's name that read "rips mended free."

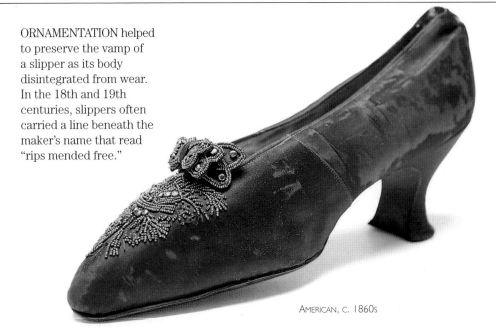

AMERICAN, C. 1860S

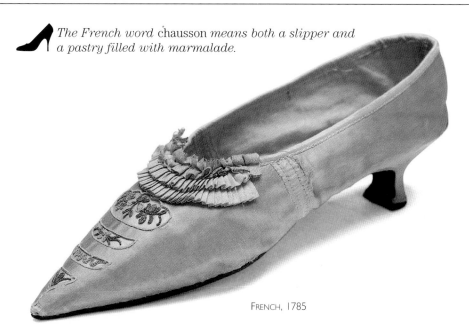

The French word chausson *means both a slipper and a pastry filled with marmalade.*

FRENCH, 1785

FOR FASHION CRITIC
Holly Brubach, Vivier's
shoes evoke "a Disney-
like image of tiny fairy
hands embroidering satin
with threads of gold,
of squirrels scurrying
through the forest bear-
ing a cargo of faceted
gold beads, of bluebirds
with satin ribbons in
their beaks, swooping and
circling around a fairy tale
heroine's ankles, tying the
final bow."

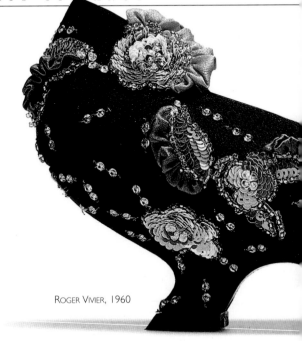

ROGER VIVIER, 1960

In fairy tales, shoes are often the vehicle of escape from humdrum lives.

FASHION WAS AT ITS most sumptuous during La Belle Epoque, a time of rarefied tastes, when a Parisian aristocrat might be seen sipping champagne from a lady's slipper. Finely embroidered silk lisle stockings (facing page) complemented lustrous silken slippers, drawing attention to the ankle.

JOSEPH BOX, 1875

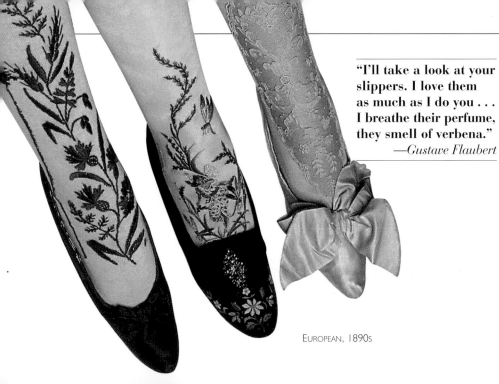

"I'll take a look at your slippers. I love them as much as I do you . . . I breathe their perfume, they smell of verbena."
—*Gustave Flaubert*

EUROPEAN, 1890s

NOT MEANT TO BE walked on, the soles of Chinese slippers for bound feet were often as elaborately embroidered as the tops.

CHINESE, 1900

ROLLER-PRINTED slippers were an inexpensive alternative to embroidered ones, which were perceived as ostentatious both in England and on the Continent after the French Revolution.

ENGLISH,
19TH CENTURY

TRICOLOR ROSETTES
on a pair of mules
embody the spirit of
the French Revolution.

FRENCH, 1789

PFISTER'S CHIC MULE, called "My Fair Lady," plays with the light-hearted informality of polka dots and gingham.

ANDREA PFISTER, 1992

I f Diana Vreeland, the high priestess of fashion, hadn't encouraged a young set designer from Switzerland to "do shoes," the Blahnik name might never have appeared on the most sought-after designs of the moment— sexy, sumptuous slippers, mules and pumps whipped up from the richest jewel-encrusted brocades, velvets and glacé kidskins. Madonna buys Blahniks ("They last longer than sex"), as do Bianca Jagger, Princess Diana and Paloma Picasso, who appreciate not only the consummate workmanship and cheeky charm of his creations but also their legendary flattering fit.

Coral necklace mule, 1980s

"I have certain little tricks," Blahnik says. "I'm king of the

Baroque slipper, 1995

Manolo Blahnik

scissors." And he has used those scissors to create such whimsical designs as a shoe meant to look like a glove and one with a strap that resembles a snake winding round the ankle. Often he borrows from other eras—a Regency heel here, a rococo vamp there—but his hand-finished shoes are as thoroughly modern as the well-heeled women who buy them.

Teardrop pearls on a slide, 1980s

Each Blahnik shoe, with its signature tapered vamp, goes through about 50 different production processes, so his factory in Parabiago, Italy, turns out only about 80 pairs a day. Such limited supply, however, seemingly makes the faithful want them all the more. One customer typically buys 23 pairs a season by phone,

sight unseen. "Blahnik is the Luther Vandross of shoes," says designer Bernard Figueroa, because his shapes are so "smooth and seductive."

Born in the Canary Islands in 1942 to a Czech father and Spanish mother, Manolo Blahnik studied literature and architecture at the

Mule with knotted vamp, 1980s

University of Geneva with set design as his goal. He dabbled in shoe design in the '70s, creating his own version of men's saddle shoes, and after his fateful meeting with Vreeland turned his attention to women's shoes. He opened his first boutique in London in 1973 and made plastic sandals called "jellies" for Fiorucci before devoting himself to more sophisticated styles. To this day, Blahnik carves heels himself and oversees

"Eos," 1995

each design manufactured at his Italian factory. His
shoes appear in top runway collections, including
those of Isaac Mizrahi, Todd Oldham and Badgley-
Mischka, as well as in the world's most glamorous
fashion magazines.

"Medina," 1995

Blahnik's earliest shoe memory is of a high-heeled Marlene
Diėtrich walking across the desert in the movie *Morocco,* and he
still conjures up characters from movies and books to inspire
his lines. After all, he says, he's creating not shoes but
"fleeting moments" imbued with the
kind of devil-may-care fantasy
even a sand-kicking
Dietrich could
appreciate.

"Lissio," 1995

OVERSIZE BOWS
dominate a pair of late
19th-century shoes,
suitable for
afternoon tea.

AMERICAN, 1880

PHILIPPE MODEL'S slippers belong to the magical fairy tale tradition, evoking a nearly lost world of innocence, caprice, and romance.

PHILIPPE MODEL, 1980s

KILIM WEAVING,
a specialty in Western
Turkey, results in excep-
tionally fine hand-woven
reversible textiles. These
women's "house shoes"
were all crafted from
kilim tapestry imported
for a European market
in the mid 19th century,
after the close of the
Crimean War.

European, 1850s

GOLD LACE BRAIDING
hand-stitched on a pair
of kid mules must have
glowed seductively in
the flickering gaslight of
19th-century parlors.

GERMAN, C. 1880

THE "CARMEN" slipper,
designed by Rankins after
a trip to Madrid, reflects
the fiery energy of the
flamenco style.

SCOTT RANKINS, 1995

PARISIAN BOTTIER
Louis Hellstern was
renowned for his extrava-
gantly decorated vamps,
here dotted with steel cut
beads and rhinestones.

HELLSTERN & SONS, 1920s

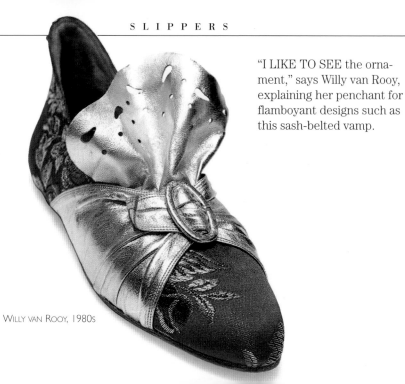

"I LIKE TO SEE the orna-
ment," says Willy van Rooy,
explaining her penchant for
flamboyant designs such as
this sash-belted vamp.

WILLY VAN ROOY, 1980s

MOROCCAN, 1980s

SUSAN BENNIS
WARREN EDWARDS, 1989

A NEAR EASTERN style of slipper (facing page), cut from sateen brocade and decorated with glass beads, was designed for both casual and formal wear. Glass beads and rhinestones turn an evening slipper from Bennis Edwards (near left) into a walking jewelry box.

The mule in its modern incarnation has long been associated with female glamour and sex appeal—especially when trimmed with the soft stork feathers known as marabou. A kind of backless slipper, the mule is the only shoe that

Mail-order marabou

leaves the foot half dressed and half undressed. And once a heel was added, the naked back of a woman's foot was placed on a pedestal and exposed as highly erotic. Mules, and in particular the marabou mule, became the de rigueur shoe in the bedroom.

In a climactic scene in *Madame Bovary,* Flaubert uses Emma's pink satin mule as a metaphor for seduction: "And when she sat on her knees, the dainty shoe was held on only by the toes of her bare foot." The design of these shoes not only allows a woman to balance them coquettishly on her toes, but also forces her to change her walk to a sex-kittenish mince—a fact that was not lost on Hollywood. In films of the '50s, marabou mules signaled steamy perdition. Marilyn Monroe strutted her stuff in them in *The Seven Year Itch.* Paparazzi snapped Mamie Van Doren and Diana Dors wearing them to the supermarket. A buyer for Frederick's of Hollywood saw a marabou mule with a 3½-inch heel in a Parisian fashion show and had it copied for the catalogue, where it still appears.

These days, marabou mules are again worn mostly as boudoir slippers, and as such they seem to have found their perfect role. As humorist Mimi Pond once observed, the only way a man can respond to a woman dressed in marabou mules is either "va-va-va voom" or "babyohbabyohbaby!"

Powder puff mule in boudoir black

DAVID EVINS, 1963

SILVER SEQUINS and jet beads topped off gold brocade mules designed for Elizabeth Taylor to wear in *Cleopatra* (facing page). This rococo damask mule was undoubtedly worn by a French coquette, her foot cruelly squeezed into its pointed toe.

FRENCH, C. 1730

A LOOSENED SHOE,
as 18th-century French
paintings suggest, implied
a loose woman. Since
mules often slid off
stockinged feet, they were
fashioned with everything
from ribbons to elastic
loops and ankle straps to
keep them in place.

FRENCH, C. 1885

PFISTER'S MULES have been called "walking post-cards." The spun-gold "Topkapi," gleaming with paste gems, is an ode to Turkish opulence.

ANDREA PFISTER, 1993

BRITISH DESIGNER Emma Hope's witty "regalia for feet" are deliciously decadent versions of men's evening slippers. A tracery of embroidery defines a glittering galaxy and flaming hearts (facing page). Sumptuous Midas-touch detailing on the vamp of this slipper recalls the hem of an Indian wedding sari.

EMMA HOPE, 1990s

EMMA HOPE, 1990s

METALLIC BEADWORK,
here on plush velvet, was
a Hellstern hallmark in
the 1920s, when Paris
was the center of world
fashion.

HELLSTERN & SONS, 1921

GOLD BRAID and tassels added to metallic and silk embroidery characterized the Eastern look adopted by French fashions in the latter half of the 19th century.

J.A. PETIT, 1873

CURLED-UP TOES, though they have no purpose, are traditional in Turkey. Back-less slippers, however, have a practical function: they're easy to slip off before entering a house of worship, where shoes are forbidden.

TURKISH, 1980s

The curved Turkish toe dates from the 12th century, when its length was regarded as a yardstick of the wearer's wealth. At the height of this trend, shoes measured up to 30 inches from heel to toe.

TURKISH, 1980S

THE "SMILEY FACE" and m/f logo on the vamps of these mass-produced slippers exemplify Japan's penchant for appropriating American pop culture imagery.

JAPANESE, 1980s

IV. PUMP & CIRCUMSTANCE:
THE LITTLE BLACK DRESS OF SHOES

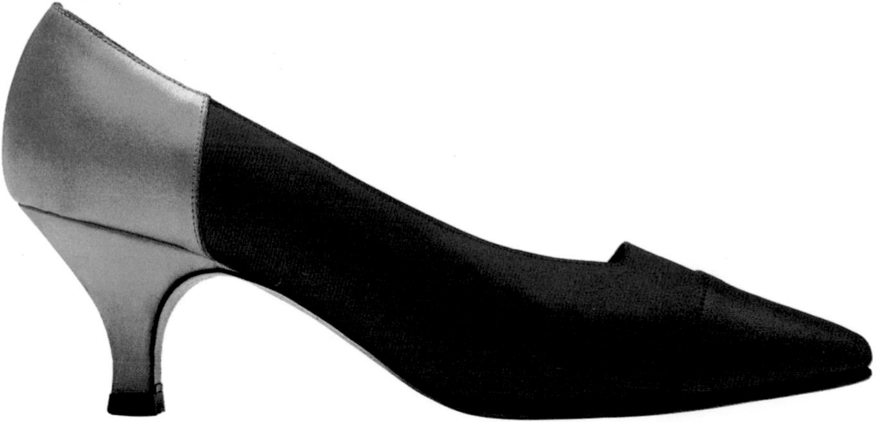

lways in style, the pump is the little black dress of the shoe world. In its pure, unadorned form, with a sensible heel, it is practical, elegant, well-bred and classically conservative.

Nowadays the pump is essentially a woman's shoe, but in the early 16th century it was part of a footman's uniform—a flat, flimsy slipper that needed to be gripped in place with the heel and toe muscles. Its name, first used in 1555 and spelled *poumpe, pompe* or *pumpe,* derived from the sound the shoe made when it hit a polished floor.

Women first adopted this heel-less shoe in the mid 1700s, adapting it from a street version favored by dandies, and it quickly took hold in Europe as an alternative to the impractical slipper and constricting laced boot. By century's end, after the invention of patent leather, pumps showed up on both sides of the Atlantic on the feet of ladies and gentle-

Originally adopted from men's footwear, the pump still enjoys a state of simple unadornment. This page: Fausto Santini, 1995. Preceding page: Jimmy Choo, 1990s.

men who considered them *the* shoes to dance in.

Gradually outgrowing their unisex image, pumps began to acquire heels. Bows prettied their vamps; ornate buckles lent an air of elegance. Around 1838, Alfred Gabriel, the Count d'Orsay, literally took the pump in hand and tailored it for women. His shoe was a daring departure from the closed court shoe of the era. Its V-shaped

Swiss barrette pump, 1874

vamp skimmed the cleavage of the toes, and its cutaway sides revealed the arch of the foot. Cut from black or tan kidskin and carrying a sensible 2-inch heel, the d'Orsay pump was a staple in every turn-of-the-century wardrobe. And to this day its distinctive silhouette remains a perennial fashion shape for women's shoes.

When the racy high heels of the Jazz Age gave way to moderation, pumps returned to their senses—but not for long. In the 1950s, when 4-inch stilettos held sway, Coco Chanel collaborated

Joseph Magnin, 1962

with Raymond Massaro and subversively launched a low-heeled pump. Two-toned with a sling-back, its beige body and heel optically extended the line of the leg while its black toe cap made the foot appear smaller.

In 1955 Givenchy introduced the low-heeled opera pump, cut straight across the instep with a back quarter whose sides slanted down toward the vamp. When fashion arbiter Babe Paley teamed it with cashmere sweater sets and strands of pearls, the pump gained aristocratic chic. In the '60s Jacqueline Kennedy set the style in the White House and elsewhere with her tailored suits, pillbox hats and classy pumps. And every President's wife since has adopted the pump as a hallmark of respectability and good taste.

Chanel, 1994

Robert Clergerie, 1996

First feet (from left to right): Barbara Bush, Nancy Reagan, Rosalynn Carter, Betty Ford, Pat Nixon, Lady Bird Johnson

When women entered the workforce in great numbers in the 1980s and '90s, they demanded fashionable shoes that could be worn comfortably all day. And manufacturers responded with broader toes, a wider range of sizes and widths, and a lower 1½-inch heel. Ferragamo's "Vara" pump and Vivier's "Pilgrim" combined comfort and sophisticated good looks. As Manhattan foot specialist Mayde Lebensfeld says of the contemporary pump: "The shoe fits—and finally we can wear it."

IN THE '50s, Margaret
Jerrold (a husband-and-
wife team) originated
a line of low-heeled
sophisticated shoes that
competed with stiletto
styles. A velvet heel and
straw-thin strips of velvet
ribbon produced a stream-
lined pump of tailored
elegance.

MARGARET JERROLD, 1955

**"We shall walk in velvet shoes:
Wherever we go
Silence will fall like dews
On white silence below."**
—*Elinor Wylie*

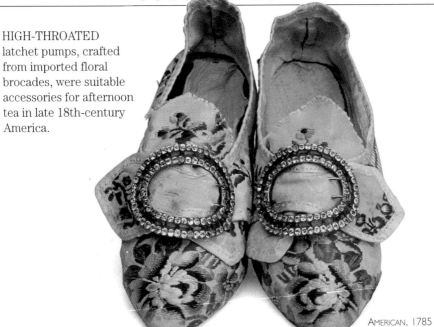

HIGH-THROATED latchet pumps, crafted from imported floral brocades, were suitable accessories for afternoon tea in late 18th-century America.

AMERICAN, 1785

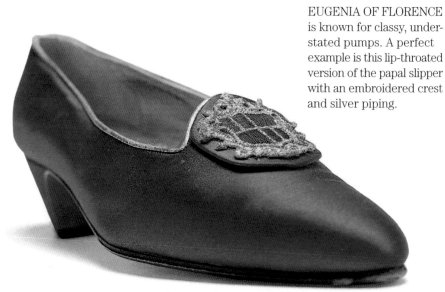

EUGENIA OF FLORENCE is known for classy, understated pumps. A perfect example is this lip-throated version of the papal slipper with an embroidered crest and silver piping.

EUGENIA OF FLORENCE, 1988

A COURT IN MOURNING
following the death of
Albert, Queen Victoria's
beloved prince consort,
lent authority and long-
lasting stature to
the basic black
pump.

In the 1880s and '90s it was unseemly for a lady to bring undue attention to herself in public. Rules of "appropriate" attire dictated dark-colored shoes.

AMERICAN, 1895

AMERICAN, 1890

SWISS, 1904

BUILDING ON the success
of his father's tailored style,
Roland Jourdan took the
basic pump, elongated the
toe and saddled it with
the simplest of buckles.

JOURDAN, 1950s

GLORIFYING the mundane, Verin draws inspiration for her designs from everyday objects—here a piano keyboard and the markings of a New York City Checker cab.

HELENE VERIN, 1979

"THE MOST EXPENSIVE custom shoemaker in the world," claimed the sign outside Yantorny's Paris salon. A former curator of shoes at the Cluny Museum, Yantorny crafted exquisite shoes from alligator and other exotic skins.

YANTORNY, 1920s

VIVIER'S DECORATIVE urge found an outlet even in his moderate-heeled pumps. This sleek silk shantung pump with black eyelet was designed for Drue Heinz, the ketchup heiress.

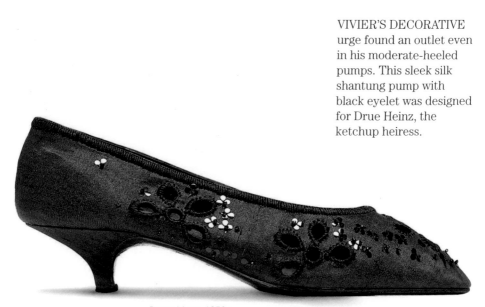

ROGER VIVIER, 1950s

BALLY, 1914

BALLY, 1914

BALLY, 1891

FROM ITS HUMBLE beginnings in a Swiss village in 1851, the Bally Shoe Company came to rival the most famous factories of France, England and America. These high-vamped pumps with curved heels and intricate detail show off the elegance of the Bally style.

A SHOWMAN as well as a shoeman, Herman Delman used film stars in his ads and was one of the first manufacturers to insist that his name appear with the store name on shoe labels. Decades later, his company still wins respect for its classic styling.

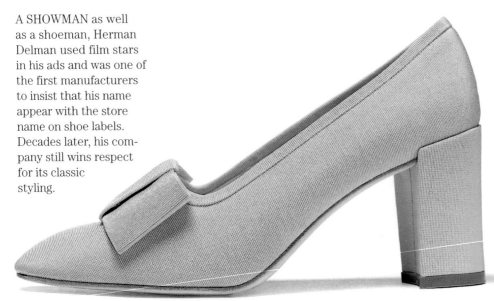

DELMAN, 1995

BLAHNIK HAS WON a place in the hearts of fashion editors—in part because his superb sense of proportion can make even a model's size 10 foot look dainty and sexy. This courtly pump has a low block heel and rhinestone buckle.

MANOLO BLAHNIK, 1990S

IN THE 1920s, the house
of Pinet was creating
T-strap eveningwear,
like this salmon-colored
pump embroidered with
point de chainette, for
the Parisian smart set.

PINET, 1920s

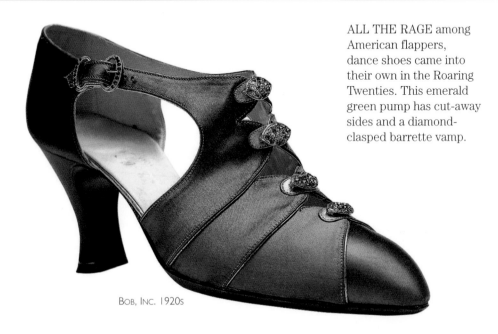

ALL THE RAGE among American flappers, dance shoes came into their own in the Roaring Twenties. This emerald green pump has cut-away sides and a diamond-clasped barrette vamp.

BOB, INC. 1920s

IMPROVING ON tradition,
Madrid-based designer
Sybilla replaced the classic
Mary Jane instep strap
with elastic trim and
boxed off the heel and
toe.

SYBILLA, 1995

ROGER VIVIER FOR DELMAN, 1990s

THE PILGRIM PUMP became one of fashion's most copied shoes after its first appearance in Saint Laurent's '62 collection. For two evening pumps, Vivier rounded the corners of the famous square buckle and lyricized it into a rhinestone swirl.

THE BEAUTY of the basic pump is that a simple ornament can effect a dramatic change in its personality. These 20th-century buckles can be clipped on for fun or to add a touch of pizzazz.

Throughout his 40-year career, David Evins turned out classic shoes that were as modish as they were comfortable. The wealthy and the powerful flocked to him because they recognized that he was a master of his craft. Even the demanding Duchess of Windsor, the embodiment of snobbishly good taste, routinely commissioned shoes from him and hailed him as a genius. He shod every President's wife from Mamie Eisenhower on and designed both pairs of Nancy Reagan's Inaugural pumps.

Movie stars loved him because his creations embodied their own personalities as much as the characters they were

Quilted pump, 1950s

Audrey Hepburn's brocade "Sabrina" pump, 1963

Evins, left, in his New York factory

meant to portray. He created glamorous mules for Ava Gardner, clunky pumps for his favorite dinner date, Judy Garland, and leopard skin bootees for the aloof Marlene Dietrich, as well as the low-heeled pumps Grace Kelly wore when she married Prince Rainier.

At the age of 13, Evins immigrated to the United States from England and went on to study illustration at the Pratt Institute in Brooklyn. He found his métier as a shoe designer after being fired from *Vogue* (an editor said his shoe renderings "reeked of artistic license"), when he went to work as a pattern maker. His talents rapidly developed, and in 1941 he

Rhinestone "Stop and Go" mules for Ava Gardner, 1955

secured a contract with I. Miller to produce his own label. Eight
years later the fashion industry presented "the King
of Pumps" with a coveted Coty Award for his
décolleté shell pumps. Other innovations fol-
lowed. Evins secured halter-backed sandals with Velcro and was the first
designer to dye alligator in vivid colors like turquoise. He dismantled
trophies and transformed their stems into heels, and like Ferragamo before him he fashioned vamps from fishing line.
An unassuming man, Evins abhorred
fussiness and unnecessary ornamentation.
"Sheer simplicity is my forte," he
told *Footwear News* in

Conservative pumps for the
Duchess of Windsor, both 1970s

1987. "It's not what you put on but what you take off"—a philosophy reflected in the refinement of his creations. He himself was usually buttoned into a Turnbull & Asser shirt and Charvet tie when he sat in his factory sewing his own shoes or carving lasts alongside his frock-coated employees.

"He was wonderfully contradictory," remembers his nephew Reed Evins, who currently designs for Cole-Haan. "He was an absolute perfectionist who'd fly into a rage and reject 300 pairs of shoes if their black satin uppers contained a tinge too much gray. On the other hand, he was anything but a prima donna. He was always floored when he won an award. He'd stand in the middle of the factory looking stunned and say, 'No kidding?' "

Mosaic embossed leather and whimsical Turkish toe dress up the pump.

For Grace Kelly, a twisted pearl sandal, 1959

HEMLINES DROPPED
to mid-calf in the '30s,
and instep-hugging heels
with high vamps and
rounded toes completed
the conservative look.

DELMAN,
1930s

HOOLE KNOWLES & CO.,
1930s

DRESS SILHOUETTES of the '50s ranged from "Hourglass" to "A-line," and shoes followed suit. But whether its heel was waisted, squat, spool-shaped or spiked, the '50s pump was always feminine.

SAKS FIFTH AVENUE, 1954

THE TWO-TONE PUMP, created by Raymond Massaro for Chanel in 1957, has appeared every season since—only its heel and toe shapes have changed to reflect each decade's dress silhouettes. In the '90s, the Chanel classic is available in seven heel heights ranging from flat to stilettos.

RAYMOND MASSARO, 1957

KARL LAGERFELD, 1990s

KARL LAGERFELD, 1990s

PERUGIA'S PUMPS, characterized by their superb elegance, reveal his flair for mixing and matching materials such as silk, snakeskin and metal mesh.

ANDRÉ PERUGIA, 1930s

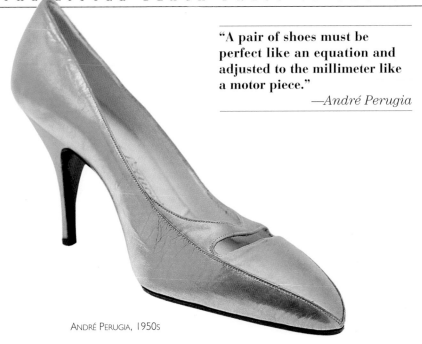

"A pair of shoes must be perfect like an equation and adjusted to the millimeter like a motor piece."

—*André Perugia*

ANDRÉ PERUGIA, 1950s

COMFORTABLE YET handsome, this high-cut Ferragamo pump alternates calf and suede in a style that was very fashionable for daywear in the late '20s.

SALVATORE FERRAGAMO, 1928

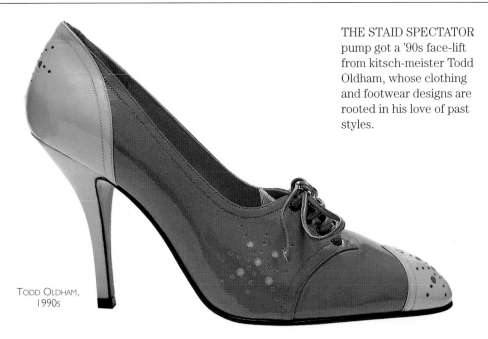

THE STAID SPECTATOR
pump got a '90s face-lift
from kitsch-meister Todd
Oldham, whose clothing
and footwear designs are
rooted in his love of past
styles.

TODD OLDHAM,
1990s

Around 1822 American cobblers created the first "left" and "right" shoes, using two lasts. These shoes, called "crookeds," vastly improved comfort.

DIEGO DELLA VALLE, 1990s

ROBERT CLERGERIE, 1996

"SIMPLICITY is my one principle," says Clergerie. "When you start over-decorating, you have no strong idea." The sophistication of his sling-back resides in its pure line. A gently squared toe softens Della Valle's loafer pump (facing page).

MORE THAN ANY other color, red shoes have always had a powerful aura. In Hans Christian Andersen's tale *The Red Shoes* they drove the heroine to dance her way to death. In *The Wizard of Oz*, they were the heroine's salvation.

VIVIENNE WESTWOOD, 1995

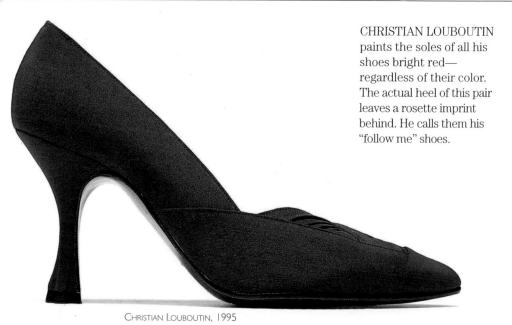

CHRISTIAN LOUBOUTIN paints the soles of all his shoes bright red—regardless of their color. The actual heel of this pair leaves a rosette imprint behind. He calls them his "follow me" shoes.

CHRISTIAN LOUBOUTIN, 1995

EVEN UNDERSTATED,
a Model shoe shows the
hand of a master. His blue
silk pump has a soft self
bow and an elegant
museum heel.

PHILIPPE MODEL, 1980s

AS READY-TO-WEAR designers began licensing everything from sheets to shoes, the Anne Klein company hired top-notch designers—including Manolo Blahnik in the '90s. This silk pump with its ruched vamp and Sabrina heel typifies the label.

ANNE KLEIN II, 1990s

CLEAN AND ELEGANT
lines characterize a
Clergerie pump. The com-
fortable, slipper-like fit of
this style comes from its
generous toe box and
anatomically forgiving last.

ROBERT CLERGERIE, 1996

FIAMMA FERRAGAMO, Salvatore's heir, made a splash in the late '70s with the "Vara" pump, which has sold over a million pairs. Its sporty low heel, comfortable fit and signature gold-toned plaque give the shoe instantly recogniz-able status in the '90s.

FERRAGAMO, 1996

THE ANKLE-STRAP pump, no matter the decade or designer, will always exemplify the Twenties—an era of speakeasies, wild parties and dance marathons.

DELMAN, 1920S

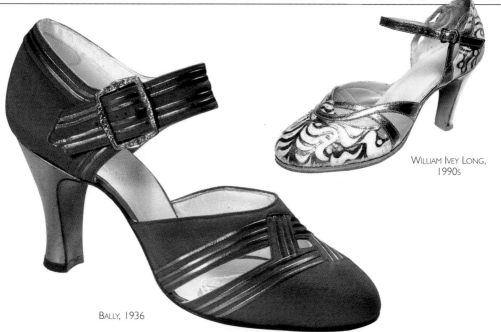

WILLIAM IVEY LONG,
1990s

BALLY, 1936

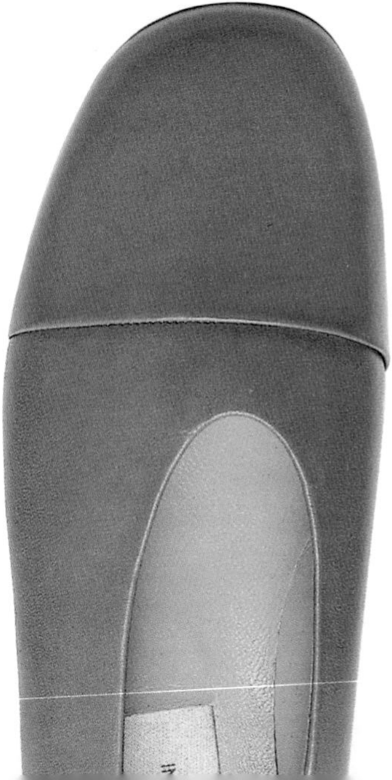

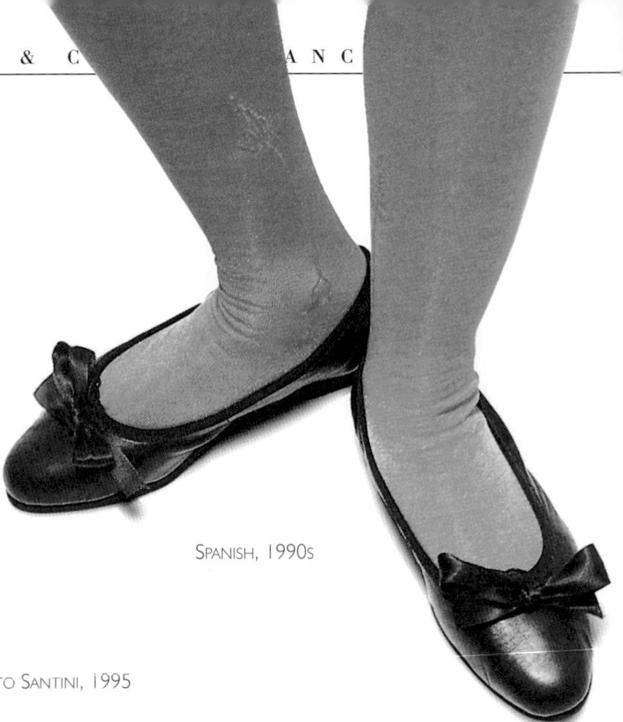

Spanish, 1990s

Fausto Santini, 1995

A-LINE, 1995

THE UPS AND DOWNS of fashion notwithstanding, some women have always favored low shoes. These classic flats, with their "baby doll" toes, recall the *zapatillas* (center) worn with pink stockings in the bullring.

ANDRÉ COURRÈGES was one of the first ready-to-wear designers to put his name to footwear. This flat Mary Jane, with its punchy color and exaggerated squared toe and tongue, was a perfect accompaniment to his futuristic frocks.

ANDRÉ COURRÈGES, 1968

Childhood's classic slipper is the Mary Jane—the flat, blunt-toed, single-strapped party shoe that signals a child's transition from baby to little girl or boy. Named for a character in the "Buster Brown" comic strip, which first appeared in the New York *Herald* in 1902, the simple style has changed little over the years. Shirley Temple skipped across the screen in a white pair in *Baby Takes a Bow* in 1934; John Kennedy, Jr., saluted his father's passing casket in them nearly 30 years later.

The favorite material for Mary Janes has been and remains shiny black patent, but the single strap is what defines the style, acting almost like training wheels on a bike to prepare little girls for their first pair of strapless pumps. Not until the '60s did they move

T-strap Mary Jane,
un matin d'eté, 1996

from the schoolyard to the atelier. In the "youthquake" of that era, traditional couture was abandoned in favor of fashion that both celebrated innocence and turned its youthful images into something more politically and sexually charged. British designer Mary Quant flaunted stodgy convention by putting woman-child Twiggy in an art smock and shodding her in black tap shoes. In Paris, Courrèges outfitted his models in minitunics, baby bonnets and round-toed flats with a buttoned strap and broad tongue. Betsey Johnson, designing for Paraphernalia in New York, paired minidresses, inspired by the dance costumes she wore in elementary school, with flats whose strap sat high on the instep. British *Vogue* acknowledged this baby-doll boom, writing of "the secret rouging of knees above white socks."

Bally, 1904

Decades later, the trend was revived as part of the "waif" look of the early '90s. New nymphets, notably Kate Moss, sported shrunken T-shirts, sheer Sunday school dresses and shiny Mary Janes sold by everyone from Gucci to J. Crew to Doc Martens. But out of context, without the political references of the '60s, the trend seemed merely to infantilize women.

Peter Fox's 1994 "Toddler" shoe, a close-vamped Mary Jane inspired by a 19th-century baby's slipper, was criticized by the press as the season's most condescending accessory. Fox responded by saying that he was simply paying tribute to the comfort and innocence of children's shoes.

On the other hand, young women such as singer

Peter Fox's "Toddler," 1994

Courtney Love, who claims to have invented the look that she calls

Hedi Raikamo, 1990

"kinderwhore," used this kiddie-based fashion to send an entirely different message. By reappropriating these little-girl images, she and others turned them into an ironic symbol of post-feminist empowerment.

The latest incarnation of the Mary Jane, as interpreted by Calvin Klein in 1996, is set on a high, chunky heel and features a low, elongated vamp and a thin strap. Somehow it succeeds in combining the simplicity and innocence of childhood with a grown-up elegance.

Maud Frizon, 1980s

THE MARY JANE is a
footwear changeling.
Bennis Edwards' cheeky
version of the classic is
upholstered in chintz.

Susan Bennis Warren Edwards, 1993

V. THE SENSIBLE SHOE:
THESE SHOES ARE MADE FOR . . .

Dutch klomp, 1996

The early brogue, the original clog, the Native American moccasin and the simple Egyptian sandal are the only styles of footwear we actually need. The rest are shoemakers' dreams and the fulfillment of women's (and men's) fantasies. When design is driven by function, not fashion, the sensible shoe—a triumph of fit over frivolity—is the welcome result. Even playful or more fashion-oriented adaptations of sensible shoes retain their integrity of purpose, providing the freedom and comfort to stride rather than mince or totter through life.

Above: hand-beaded Native American moccasin, 1890s. Preceding page: Glacée, 1995.

The majority of comfortable women's styles are derived from men's footwear. The oxford and the brogue, the ghillie and the yachting shoe, the sneaker and the running shoe—all were made first for men and later adapted for the female foot.

Other sturdy designs like the Native American moccasin, the clog and the espadrille were unisex from the start.

Practicality, not vanity, inspired the creation of the Native American deerskin moccasin, one of the earliest unisex shoes and the precursor of the contemporary loafer. These soft one-piece "foot bags" wrapped up and over the feet, providing protection from the elements and increased mobility. Colonial women, their feet enslaved by confining, toe-pinching European-style shoes, quickly recognized the moccasin's benefits and some adopted them for indoor wear. In Europe, footwear would continue to reflect class distinctions. Rural and working-class women had always worn sensible

Chanel espadrilles, 1995

shoes, while their cossetted upper-class counterparts were imprisoned by impractical but beautiful styles that reflected privileged, indolent lives. Although it was socially acceptable for upper-class women to wear riding boots and other sensible sports-related footwear, more than 200 years would pass before most women took comfort seriously.

A period of rapid social and economic change beginning in the mid 1800s changed women's lives and, consequently, the way they dressed. The parallel women's suffrage and dress reform movements encouraged women to exercise their rights as individuals and to exorcise constricting fashions in favor of "health, comfort and beauty." As women began to work outside the home in offices and factories, their shoes and clothing became less confining and more practical. The broad-heeled "commonsense" shoes favored by suffragettes on protest marches became fashionable for recreational walking, and more women began actively participating in sports, their feet comfortably shod in canvas and rubber athletic boots or "sneakers." By the 1920s, women's bodies were liberated and so were their feet. Adaptations of men's footwear styles such as the brogue, the ghillie and the oxford proliferated.

Canvas and leather sports boot designed by Sharlot Battin for the 1994 play Vita and Virginia

Snub-toed patent-leather oxford, Jan Jansen, 1994

World War II, as did World War I, found women stepping out of fashion and into sturdy shoes or boots as they replaced men on assembly lines.

The oxford itself found its greatest champion in America's First Lady, Eleanor Roosevelt, who wore her no-nonsense Cuban-heeled oxfords with a plain silk frock. But context creates its own meaning, and the wearer indelibly imprints her personality on her attire.

Child's saddle oxford, Buster Brown, c. 1950

While Eleanor looked stodgy and determined in her oxfords, Katharine Hepburn and Marlene Dietrich managed to look enigmatic, daring and comfortable in theirs. Commandeering men's suits and severely tailored women's wear, these two gender-benders achieved a chic, slouchy look that made a strong statement about comfort and freedom. The effect was totally glamorous and a bit eccentric with undertones of sexual blending that did not draw the line at footwear. Their oxford-clad feet became the last word in insouciant stylishness.

Pointed-toe sneaker, 1950s

MOCCASINS were the earliest foot coverings worn in North America. Soft and flexible, the one-piece construction of deerskin moccasins permitted swift, easy movement. Decorative shells, colorful beads and dyed porcupine quills were attached in designs unique to each tribe.

Moccasin-like "foot bags" were worn in northern Europe as early as the Bronze Age.

IROQUOIS, C. 1820

MANY COLONIAL women abandoned hard-soled shoes in favor of moc-casins, especially for indoor wear. Native American seamstresses tailored moccasins to this new market by adding fabric lining and silk ribbon ties.

EASTERN SIOUX, C. 1880

FOR SIX CENTURIES, until about 1915, the plain, durable and inexpensive wooden clog was the everyday shoe of the masses in northern Europe. Dress-up clogs painted with flowers and the owner's initials were worn on Sundays and feast days in 19th-century Holland.

DUTCH, 1800s

DANSKO, 1996

TODAY many European and American chefs wear generously padded Danish-style clogs with leather uppers for protection from splattering food. Molded polyurethane soles based on the traditional wooden designs are comfortable and help prevent skidding on kitchen floors as chefs dash from one work area to another.

RUBBER SOLES were joined to low-cut, lace-up canvas uppers by the 1860s, creating the genteel "croquet sandal" worn by the idle rich. The democratically priced Ked, introduced by U.S. Rubber in 1917, was the first popularly marketed sneaker. The name combined the Latin *ped-*, "foot," with a "K" for "kid."

KEDS, 1996

The average person walks 2,000 miles a year.

THE ALL STAR by Converse, which debuted in 1919, had bootlike high tops and was made of serviceable, no-nonsense tan canvas with brown rubber soles. It was the forerunner of athletic shoes for both sexes.

CONVERSE ALL STAR,
1923

THE FIRST NIKES hit the market in 1971. Named for the Greek winged goddess of victory, they featured innovative "waffle" soles, wedged heels, cushioning and nylon uppers.

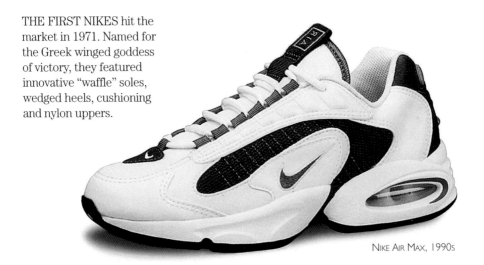

NIKE AIR MAX, 1990s

Running shoes became acceptable streetwear when thousands of women walked to work in suits and sneakers during the 1980 New York City transit strike.

REEBOK, 1996

NOBOX, 1996

REEBOK'S FREESTYLE aerobics shoe, introduced in 1982, was specifically engineered for women's feet. This and other Reebok designs inspired a high-heeled parody of practicality called Nobox in the mid '90s.

 *In pre-sneaker times, Brazilian Indians waterproofed the soles of their feet by*

FROM LEFT TO RIGHT: 1996 NIKES FOR RUNNING, CONDITIONING, TRACK AND TRAINING

dipping them in liquid latex from rubber trees.

THE AESTHETICS of athleticism turned racy in the mid '90s when sneaker soles began to sport dynamic graphics and eye-popping bursts of color. The fanciful visuals also reflected the shoes' functions: for running and conditioning, the message was motion with mesmerizing spirals and zigzag patterns; for cross-trainers, bold but less agitated patterns prevailed.

THE ORIGINAL Top-Sider was a boating shoe with a brown leather upper and traction rubber sole for gripping the deck. Yachtsman Paul Sperry modeled his patented sole after the deep, wavelike grooves in the paws of his cocker spaniel.

SPERRY TOP-SIDER,
1996

BOATING SHOES have made the transition from deckwear to streetwear with these sleek patent leather Sebagos.

SEBAGO, 1996

NONSKID DRIVING shoes worn by European sports car aficionados inspired Italian designer Diego Della Valle to create J.P. Tod's in 1979. The sole and heel of these quirky unisex moccasins are embedded with rubber pebbles designed to grip car pedals. Made in more than 100 colors, Tod's have become the status shoe of the '90s, favored by the fit and the fabulous.

DIEGO DELLA VALLE, 1996

DIEGO DELLA VALLE, 1996

THE BASS WEEJUN is the last word in tailored comfort. Similar to moccasins in construction, Weejuns are also easily slipped on and off. Their nickname "penny loafers" derived from the '50s fad of slotting a penny into the vamp.

G.H. Bass, 1996

FASHION appropriated the penny loafer and made it chic. High-heeled Chanel loafers come with their own specially minted coins.

CHANEL, 1995

VARIATIONS on the loafer are infinite. Snake-skin and tassles add elegance and a note of formality to Anne Klein's version of the familiar classic.

ANNE KLEIN, 1995

ELITE AND EXPENSIVE, the Gucci loafer in flat and stacked-heel versions was the status symbol of the ladies-who-lunch set in the 1970s. Its signature harness hardware is a miniaturized version of the real thing used by Florentine saddler Guccio Gucci.

Gucci, 1993

The best-known of England's new wave of shoe designers, Patrick Cox was christened "the Ferragamo of MTV" by the media for his imaginative yet comfort-infused footwear and the hip celebrities who collect his designs. "You don't have to walk around with blisters," Cox points out. "That's an old way

Patrick Cox, creator of the "Wannabe," surrounded by a whirlwind array of his other designs. Left: court shoe, 1990s.

"of thinking. The best compliment anyone could pay me is that they wore my shoes to death."

Born in Edmonton, Canada, Cox moved to London to study shoemaking at the prestigious Cordwainers College.

Before leaving school, he originated a brief vogue for metal-capped toes and undertook commissions from Body Map and his idol, Vivienne Westwood.

Cox's label debuted in stores in 1986, prompting instantaneous buzz about his subversively classic designs, including a simple black pump with the heel encased in a curtain of

"Moon Boot," 1994

Union Jack "Wannabe," 1996

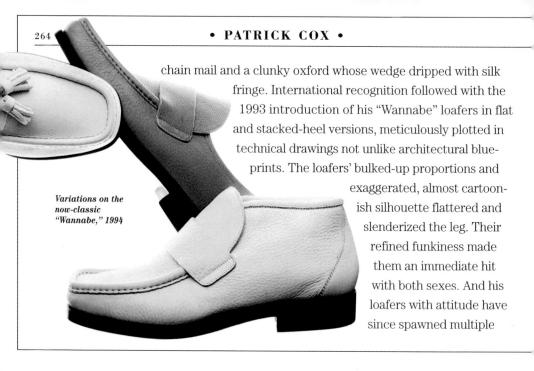

chain mail and a clunky oxford whose wedge dripped with silk fringe. International recognition followed with the 1993 introduction of his "Wannabe" loafers in flat and stacked-heel versions, meticulously plotted in technical drawings not unlike architectural blueprints. The loafers' bulked-up proportions and exaggerated, almost cartoonish silhouette flattered and slenderized the leg. Their refined funkiness made them an immediate hit with both sexes. And his loafers with attitude have since spawned multiple

Variations on the now-classic "Wannabe," 1994

Ghillie spectator pumps, 1994

imitations. Meanwhile, peripatetic Cox has created "Wannabe" clothing designs for women and men, launched a line of purses and small accessories, and collaborated on the design of what may turn out to be the next best thing to slipping into a pair of "Wannabes"—riding the "Wannabe" scooter. With retail stores in the United States, England and France, plus franchises in Australia and Japan, Cox is a trendsetter who likes to go into fashion "by the back door."

High-heeled python "Wannabe" and matching purse, 1995

HUSH PUPPIES came in with the development of brushed pigskin in the late '50s. Named for the little balls of fried cornmeal used by Southern cooks to hush up dogs in the kitchen, they were bland-looking but spectacularly comfortable. Slip-on styles were called "Earls"; the laced ones, "Dukes." In the early '90s, they took on new colors and were co-opted as cutting-edge unisex accessories.

HUSH PUPPIES, 1995

"Barking dogs" is slang for aching feet—a condition rarely experienced by those who wear Hush Puppies.

HUSH PUPPIES, 1996

THE SADDLE SHOE, made of white buckskin with a black or brown leather instep "saddle," was created for adults and children in 1910. In the '50s, on *American Bandstand,* teenage girls rocked and rolled in clunky saddle shoes and thick bobby socks that anchored their acres of crinoline.

In 1949, Buster Brown offered 37 variations on the basic saddle shoe.

G.H. BASS, 1996

ROBERT CLERGERIE, 1996

SCALE IS EVERYTHING when men's footwear successfully transcends gender. "My idea," says Clergerie, "was to make women's shoes inspired by men's shoes but with women's proportions." Supple and sophisticated, this svelte oxford has a generous comfort quotient.

NATTY TWO-TONE golf oxfords with spikes are a variation on the spectator-style shoes that were popular during the Jazz Age. They found favor among women golfers of the '30s, who appreciated their dashing lines and the note of crisp elegance they added to tailored sportswear.

HENRI BEGUELIN, 1990s

THE SPORTY SPECTATOR
was given a heel and
punched, serrated detailing
to become versatile
streetwear in the 1930s.
Lagerfeld's versions for
the 1990s, flat (far left) or
with a high heel, updated
this dashing look with
accents such as wing tips,
modified saddle-shoe vamps
and contrasting laces.

KARL LAGERFELD, 1995

They're unique, scarce and expensive. And coveted by a cult of chic comfort-seekers with lifetime standing orders to receive each new color combination as it arrives. Available only at a small shop tucked away in midtown Manhattan, the Belgian shoe's sole purveyor is Henri Bendel. Soon after selling his namesake New York department store in 1955, Bendel began importing a handmade "moc-casual," modeled after a

Left: a velvet Belgian loafer. Right: for summer, linen in every color under the sun.

Belgian felt peasant slipper. Though Bendel recently renamed it the Belgian "casual" after a spate of line-for-line imitations appeared in the mid 1990s, for many years his classic has been known as the Belgian loafer. Completely hand-made by Belgian artisans who work at home, it is built on a calfskin mini-wedge heel, the calf upper discreetly outlined with a slender strand of piping. A minuscule hand-tied leather bow accents most versions.

The Belgian casual's design has remained unchanged for more than 40 years, but ennui is not an issue. It comes in every color imaginable—in cotton or silk brocade, Belgian linen, "lizard calf," patent leather, crushed velvet or suede.

The leather lining of each shoe is meticulously attached by hand with tiny stitches.

BILLBOARDS for political statements, Di Mauro's "Liberation" shoe celebrated the end of World War II and Mayer's slipper wears the red AIDS ribbon of the 1990s (both facing page). Moschino combined the peace and love symbols of the '60s on the vamp of his '80s design.

MOSCHINO, 1980s

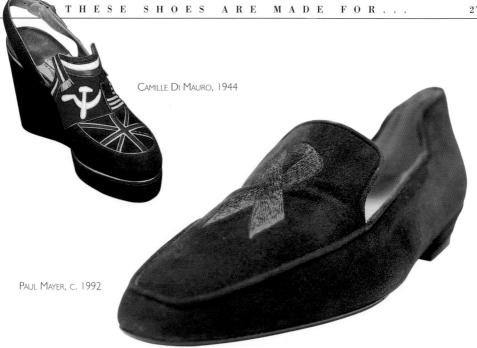

CAMILLE DI MAURO, 1944

PAUL MAYER, C. 1992

ACCORDING TO ERMA
Bombeck, "If shoes don't
hurt, they don't have
style." Maud Frizon
proves her wrong with a
sling-back wedge that's as
chic as it is comfortable.

MAUD FRIZON, 1980s

A STRETCH ELASTIC
mule, crafted by Model
from a single piece of fabric, molds to the foot like
a glove and feels like a
second skin. Civilized and
comfortable, this paceset-
ting design, introduced in
the early '90s, became
one of the decade's most
imitated styles.

PHILIPPE MODEL, 1995

TOSSING CORSETS to the winds, emancipated women in the late 19th century became active in sports, prompting the need for special flexible footwear that did not pinch their feet. The first rubber-soled canvas boots and shoes were worn for lawn tennis, croquet and leisurely nature walks.

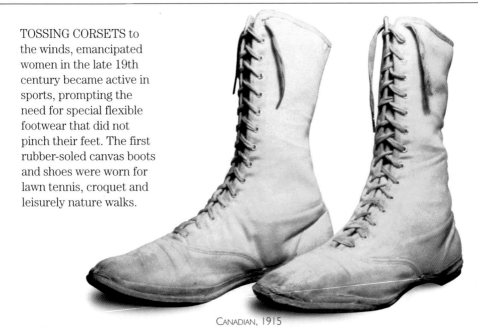

CANADIAN, 1915

NARROW-TOED bicycle boots helped novice cyclists in long skirts to search out the pedals. Panels of wool inserted in the leather calves provided ventilation, while eyelet rings at the top prevented laces from coming undone.

AMERICAN, 1895

RENEGADE English teenagers appropriated working-class Dr. Martens (aka Doc Martens) in the early 1960s, reveling in their hard-edged, aggressively utilitarian design and bulky air-cushioned soles. By the '70s male and female club kids and punk rockers around the world had discovered the boots' defiantly quirky, almost brutal simplicity.

DR. MARTENS, 1996

DOC MARTENS entered the fashion mainstream in the 1990s, inspiring sleeker, more sophisticated versions from top designers around the world.

CHARLES JOURDAN,
1996

KENZO, 1996

YANKEE INGENUITY triumphed over nature in 1911, when intrepid outdoorsman Leon Leonwood Bean, weary of slogging through Maine woods with cold, wet feet, combined the bottoms of waterproof rubber galoshes with lightweight leather tops. He sold the first 100 pairs of the Bean Boot by mail to hunting license holders. The rest is mail-order history.

L.L. BEAN, 1996

Legendary photographer Margaret Bourke-White sported a pair of L.L. Bean Maine Hunting Boots when she snapped the cover photo for the first issue of Life *magazine in 1936.*

IT TOOK DESIGNER Scott Rankins' wry sensibility to elevate the classic Bean Boot. Cheeky and waterproof, his boot made it safe for style-stalkers to go prancing in the rain.

SCOTT RANKINS, 1993

SPANISH FARMERS crafted lightweight canvas slip-ons called *alpargatas* whose soles were woven from esparto grass. By the early 1900s, at fashionable resorts on the Riviera, high society had adopted them and renamed them *espadrilles*.

EDDIE BAUER, 1996

DISPOSABLE AND CHIC, espadrilles caught on in America in the 1950s as an alternative to sandals. Joan & David's "tic-tac-toe" version is made with firm, thick woven soles designed to withstand city sidewalks.

JOAN & DAVID, 1996

BALLET SHOES are an adaptation of the fragile, unblocked, square-toed ballroom slipper of the early 1800s (top). The blocked tip of the modern toe shoe (bottom) is also stiffened with glue to support dancers *en pointe*.

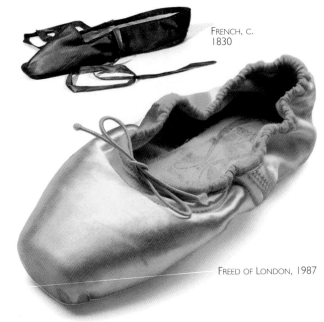

FRENCH, C. 1830

FREED OF LONDON, 1987

Movie gamine Audrey Hepburn popularized the Capezio ballet flat in 1957 as the perfect counterpoint to skinny Capri pants.

CAPEZIOS MADE the transition from stage to sidewalk in the 1940s when sportswear designer Claire McCardell asked the firm to add a hard sole. Simultaneously sexy and innocent, the low-cut "skimmer" flat reveals a demure yet daring glimpse of toe cleavage.

CAPEZIO, 1955

WIDTH IS THE KEY to
comfort and wearability.
The unusual scallop-
edged loops of the ghillie,
a design of Scottish
origin, allow the wearer
to customize the shoe's
width by tightening or
loosening the laces.

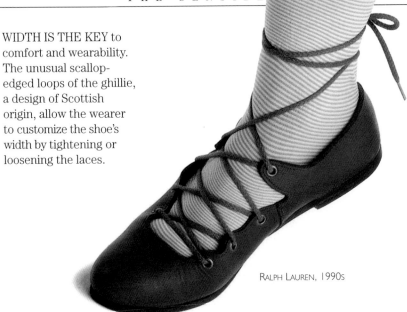

RALPH LAUREN, 1990s

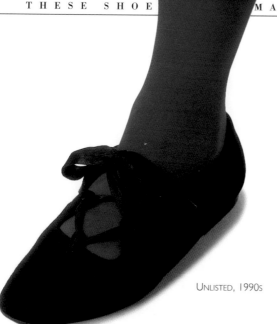

UNLISTED, 1990s

"Please do what you can. . . to liberate the captive feet of womanhood. It's not fair, and it's not fun, to hurt from the ground up in the name of fashion."
—*Abigail van Buren*
("Dear Abby")

UNISEX BIRKENSTOCKS became the counterculture's back-to-nature, antifashion statement in 1967. Their molded heel cup and patented cork, jute and natural latex "footbed" ergonomically mimic the natural contours of the foot, improving circulation and allowing toes to splay naturally. Though now made in more than 46 styles, the original twostrap "Arizona" (right) is still the best-seller.

BIRKENSTOCK, 1995

"In terms of ugliness, [Birkenstocks] are the equivalent of a gravel pit in a scenic landscape."
—*Larry Tritten*

SUSAN BENNIS
WARREN EDWARDS, 1992

CLOTHING DESIGNERS
Marc Jacobs and Randolph
Duke swept the Birken-
stock into the mainstream
in the early '90s, recogniz-
ing the clunky classic's
affinity with simple,
pared-down fashions.
Later, Susan Bennis and
Warren Edwards embel-
lished the iconic sandal
with glitzy rhinestones for
eveningwear.

PETER PAN would have envied these butter-soft pixie shoes whose foolscap points also recall a court jester's boots.

MANOLO BLAHNIK, 1980s

VI. GREAT STRIDES: THE BOOT

When Bette Midler delivered her off-the-cuff quip, "Give a girl the correct footwear and she can conquer the world," she might well have been referring to boots. Always a symbol of strength, boots also serve as talismans. In Charles Perrault's fairy tales *Puss in Boots* and *Hop o' My Thumb,* hapless victims reverse their fortune by stealing and wearing their persecutor's boots. And even General Patton observed how boots turn ordinary soldiers into warriors.

Cave paintings discovered in Spain and dated as far back as 13,000 B.C. depict both men and women wearing boots of animal skins and fur. But as the roles of the sexes became culturally entrenched, men strode forth in boots to conquer the world, while women stayed at home in slippers too delicate for anything but the boudoir. Functional footwear for women might have upset the order of things; in fact,

This page: a Bally boot from the 1880s.
Preceding page: American "afternoon boot," c. 1920.

This cuissarde was similar to the male boots worn by Joan of Arc

one of the charges against Joan of Arc, whose rebellious behavior led her to be perceived as a witch, was that she dressed in men's boots up to her thighs. In the 18th century boots had surpassed shoes as the fashionable footwear for men, yet even then upper-class women were literally kept in their place with perishable footwear made of silks and velvets.

The one exception to the rule was the equestrian boot—a scaled-down version of the men's style—that women were permitted to wear on horseback.

German galoshed half-boot, 1830

Not until the 1830s did nonworking women begin to wear boots in their daily lives. To make the female foot look daintier, the new ankle-high boots were made on narrow lasts and worn tightly laced or buttoned. They were meant to encase the flesh, removing it from temptation, but had just the opposite effect—they enhanced

*François
Pinet, 1870*

the shapeliness of the calf and proved highly erotic.

Once mass production took hold in the 1850s, boots became affordable to maids as well as the ladies they served. No longer a reliable sign of status, the boot became a symbol of emerging equality not only between the sexes, but among social groups as well.

Our own century was the first in which women's boots entered the world of fashion. New styles, materials, lengths and heel heights proliferated, and for once women who wore boots were the peacocks instead of their male counterparts. In the 1960s came the miniskirt craze, which Coco Chanel dubbed "an exhibition of meat," revealing more of a woman's leg than ever before. Suddenly boots were no longer mere accessories; they virtually dictated outfits. From low "Beatle" boots to thigh-high styles, they

*A Stephane Kélian
ghillie boot, 1980s*

stepped defiantly into the limelight, announcing women's new freedom from traditional feminine clothing.

"Kinky" boots came out of the closet and infiltrated runway fashion. Thanks in part to *Urban Cowboy*, the cowboy boot—along with workboots—was elevated from its functional status and glamorized as suddenly chic. Today Doc Martens, the quintessential unisex boots, transcend every street style, from skinhead and punk to psychobilly and grunge. And combat boots, along with Manolo Blahniks, are teamed with everything from jeans to lingerie.

It took several thousand years, but boots—once again—belong to both sexes.

Thigh-high '80s boot by Stephen Sprouse; and, right, Victoria Pratt's "Racing Boots," 1993

IN THE LAST CENTURY,
just as laced corsets
shaped a woman's torso,
tight-fitting buttoned
boots molded to her calves.
These gold kid and plush
velvet showstoppers
from the turn of the
century demonstrate
that boots had become
the height of fashion.

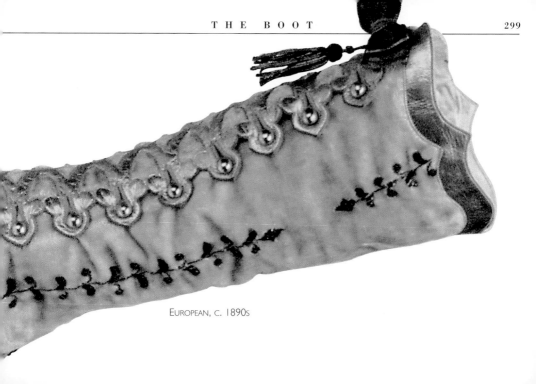

EUROPEAN, C. 1890S

WEATHERPROOF BOOTS
became one of the first
signs of female emancipa-
tion, allowing women much
greater mobility and freedom outdoors. In the ear-
liest versions, the toes of
flimsy, impractical boots,
such as these Adelaides,
were capped, or "galoshed,"
in leather.

ENGLISH, 1830s

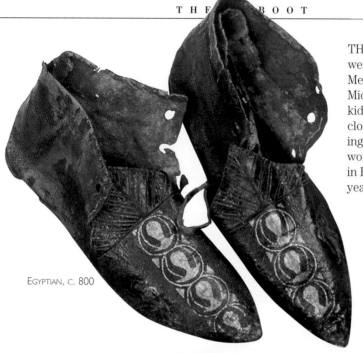

EGYPTIAN, c. 800

THE EARLIEST BOOT-wearers were the ancient Mesopotamians of the Middle East. These fine kidskin boots with laced closures and gold stenciling on the vamp were worn by Christian Copts in Egypt more than 1,000 years ago.

ONCE CONSIDERED
unflattering to the foot,
boots did not become
part of the fashionable
woman's wardrobe until
the 1830s, when a snappy
side-laced style came into
vogue. These sleeker,
more refined ankle boots
were called "Adelaides"
after the Queen Consort
of William IV.

ITALIAN, 1852

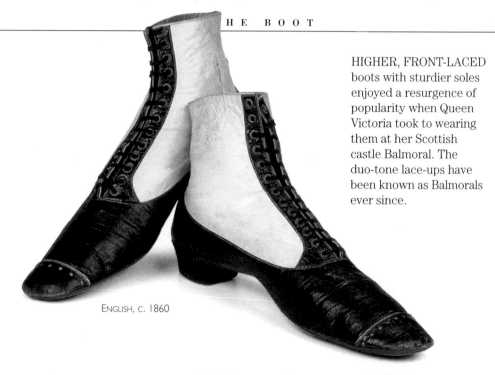

HIGHER, FRONT-LACED boots with sturdier soles enjoyed a resurgence of popularity when Queen Victoria took to wearing them at her Scottish castle Balmoral. The duo-tone lace-ups have been known as Balmorals ever since.

ENGLISH, C. 1860

IN THE GAY '90s, ornate
boots decorated with
flowers and birds were
often worn by opera-
goers and thus became
known as "opera boots."

FRANÇOIS PINET, 1890s   ITALIAN, 1880

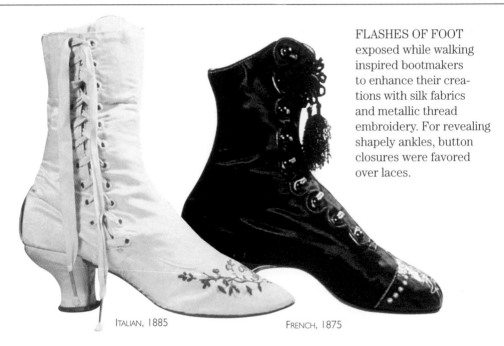

FLASHES OF FOOT
exposed while walking
inspired bootmakers
to enhance their crea-
tions with silk fabrics
and metallic thread
embroidery. For revealing
shapely ankles, button
closures were favored
over laces.

ITALIAN, 1885

FRENCH, 1875

PANT BOOTS, so named because they were designed to be worn with women's pantsuits, became popular in the '60s. David Evins fashioned these embossed alligator boots with silver kidskin for New York socialite Babe Paley.

In England in the 1950s, young mods wore "winkle-pickers"—low boots with pointed toes that looked as if they could be used to dig up sea snails, or "winkles."

DAVID EVINS, 1967

THIS SOCK BOOT from Perugia was fashioned from a stretchy fabric that hugged the ankle for a sexy effect.

ANDRÉ PERUGIA, 1930s

ELASTIC WEBBING,
made possible by Charles
Goodyear's discovery of a
method for vulcanizing rubber, allowed boots to be
quickly slipped on and off as
women's lifestyles grew
busier and more demanding.

FRENCH, 1890

FRANCELOR, 1996

ANKLE BOOTS with elastic gussets were reborn in the 1960s and became known as "Beatle boots." The mop-topped "Fab Four" wore them with their Nehru suits.

JOHN LENNON'S BOOT,
1960s

THESE WHITE BOOTS once dressed the feet of statues of saints in 18th-century Venice. The color white symbolized purity.

VENETIAN, 18TH CENTURY

FANCY COSTUME BALLS were all the rage in late 19th-century America. Women created their own costumes according to their choosen theme—in this instance, a game of dominoes.

AMERICAN, C. 1870

CHINESE SHOEMAKERS crafted the soles and basic forms of boots made for bound feet, but the beautiful embroidery was done by the women themselves. The more ornate and skillfully sewn the boot, the more highly regarded the wearer. Rose motifs symbolized longevity; bamboo, good luck; and narcissus, renewal.

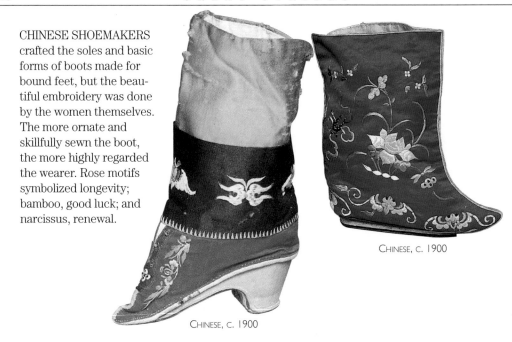

CHINESE, C. 1900

CHINESE, C. 1900

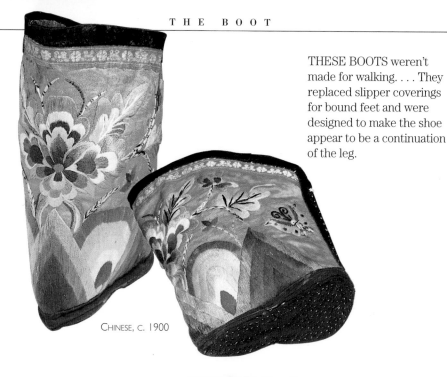

THESE BOOTS weren't made for walking. . . . They replaced slipper coverings for bound feet and were designed to make the shoe appear to be a continuation of the leg.

CHINESE, C. 1900

VICTORIAN MORALITY dictated that women's ankles be covered to protect them from men's prying eyes. Ironically, the intricate tight lacings of the ankle boots had a titillating effect.

FRANÇOIS PINET,
c.1870

FRENCH, 1890s

PEARL-AND-SILVER buttons, 17 in number, and lime-green kid added a stylish note to these otherwise practical boots with sturdy Louis heels.

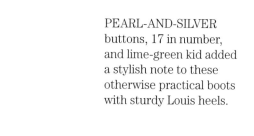 *In the 1880s, a button-hook was an essential part of every woman's wardrobe.*

EDWARD HAYES, 1880s

RIDING BOOTS for
women, unlike those for
men, have traditionally
lacked ornamentation.
Bally's soft leather and
crisp, corporate look
bring these boots out of
the sports arena.

BALLY, 1995

BALLY, 1915

WALKING BOOTS veered between the functional and the fashionable. Sensible, utilitarian boots became a cold-weather staple in the latter half of the 19th century.

In the 1860s, a typical woman's walking boot was lined with flannel, had a half-inch heel, and cost about $5.50.

CUTOUTS CAN BE both provocative and ornamental. The English "Barrette" boot from 1880 provided a playful peek at colorful stockings, while the Parisian-made satin boot (facing page, far right) was cut to reveal the ankle. The cutouts on Rankins' boot were inspired by ancient Egyptian eye icons.

ENGLISH, C. 1880

JACK JACOBUS, 1900s

SCOTT RANKINS,
1993

ADDING HEIGHT to
an ankle boot effectively
elongates the line of the
leg. Mancini's mesh ver-
sion (facing page) reveals
the arch—regarded by
some as the sexiest part
of the foot.

TODD OLDHAM, 1995

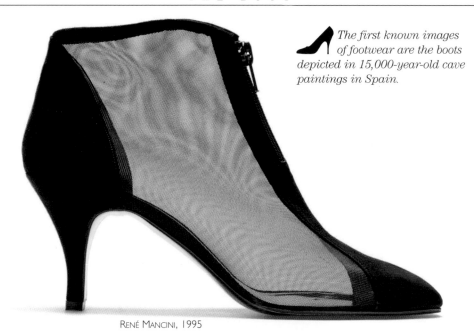

The first known images of footwear are the boots depicted in 15,000-year-old cave paintings in Spain.

RENÉ MANCINI, 1995

LISA NADING, 1994

CHARLES JOURDAN, 1988

A WELL-TURNED high heel, eye-catching trim and luxurious velvet and suede fabrics transform these boots into dashing eveningwear.

ANNE KLEIN II, 1993

BERNARD FIGUEROA, 1993   PAUL MAYER, 1984   VIVIENNE WESTWOOD, 1996

THE LARGER CANVAS that boots provide allows designers room for play. Boots this attention-getting are more than accessories; they became the focus for an entire look.

JIMMY CHOO, 1992

TWO CITY KIDS, 1990

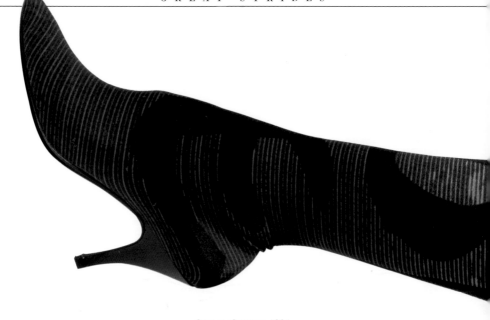

STEPHEN SPROUSE, 1984

SPROUSE silk-screened a NASA photograph of the moon on this stretchy stocking boot, then added otherworldly graffiti.

Just as the inside of a cabinet drawer reveals the woodcrafter's expertise, the sole of a customized cowboy boot measures the skill of its maker, and these days Dave Little makes the best soles in Texas. "He uses an old European process of burnishing," says authority Jim Arndt, "and it leaves the bottom of his boots as beautiful as the tops—like finely waxed floors." Little's shafts and vamps, featuring a range of skins from calf and alligator to anteater and eel, are walking testimonies to perfect craftsmanship. Then there's the legendary fit. "Never trust a custom bootmaker

Texan motif, 1995

Dave Little at work

who tells you his boots need to be broken in," says Little. "When you leave here, you should be able to forget you have anything on your feet."

A third-generation bootmaker, Little took over the San Antonio family business in 1966. Fifty years earlier, his grandfather had begun outfitting Texas ranchers with durable workboots, and by the 1940s his father was crafting flashier pairs for local cattle kings, called "saddle dandies" because of their inlaid boots with high, underslung heels. Dave Little's boots, fashioned for both women and men, feature intricately carved inlays

*A lineup from the 1996
Little catalog*

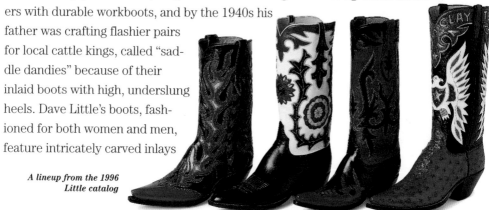

The cowboy classic

of Old West icons—longhorns, playing cards, cactuses, roses, eagles —that clearly pay homage to the classic rodeo styles of the 1920s.

A typical Little boot goes through the skilled hands of a team of 12 craftsmen using century-old methods. "Bottom men" construct the soles, stack the heel and hand-mold the pointed toes by skiving the leather with a shard of glass to make it disappear seamlessly into the vamp. "Top men" crimp the shaft, hand-stitch the collar in dense rows that hold the boot erect, then overlay a contrasting leather pattern so deftly that it appears to be painted on. By the time the finisher feather-sands, primps and polishes the boot to the luster of a new car, it has undergone more than 100 processes. "He cares about every detail and that's what makes him the best," says one Texan rancher, who preserves 25 pairs of Little boots by never wearing the same pair two days in a row.

Even though his client list must read like a *Who's Who* of Texas, Dave Little doesn't trade on the names of the famous women he's shod. "I'm not impressed by celebrities," he says. "What impresses me is a woman who recognizes a well-made boot when she sees one."

City slickers

And no matter who you are, you'll have to wait four months for a pair of boots. "That's no time to wait for something that'll last you a lifetime," says Arndt. "Little's custom boots are like pieces of finely made furniture that get better with age."

The 3/4-inch box toe

COWBOY BOOTS—
both men's and
women's—are character-
istically ornate. Turquoise
snakeskin trim and a Louis
heel give a lift to Perry's
kid boots. The 10-inch-
high "Pee Wee" style boot
is inlaid with Las Vegas
icons—hearts and dia-
monds.

MICHEL PERRY, 1995

RANCHO LOCO, 1984

THE VAMP of a Rios boot
is hand-lasted, resulting
in an excellent fit and
seamless joining of the
shaft and upper. Rios
uses calfskin because
it is lighter, thinner and
stronger than cowhide.

RIOS OF MERCEDES, 1995

MODIFIED COWBOY boots, or shoe boots, were first manufactured in the '30s for women square dancers and were later worn with jeans. In the '90s, designers like Kélian revisited and glamorized the genre.

STEPHANE KÉLIAN, 1990s

YVES SAINT LAURENT designed these elegant boots after a trip to Russia, re-creating the splendor of its artistic heritage.

YVES SAINT LAURENT, 1974

REAL SNAKESKIN—
pearlized and patch-
worked—held particular
allure in the '60s. The
pairing of materials as
disparate as leopard skin
and satin was unheard
of when Evins designed
this bootie.

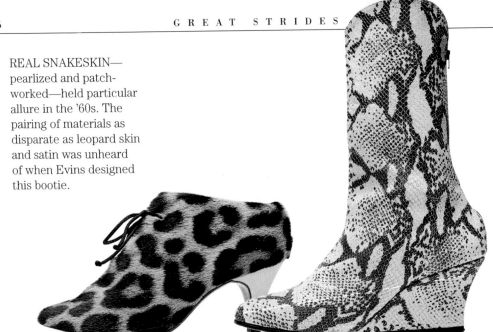

DAVID EVINS, 1960S

AMERICAN, 1960S

GIALLOMBARDO'S over-the-top boot, created from bits of fake fur trim, seems to make an animal rights statement. Delman's neatly trimmed ankle boot shows a more discreet use of leather printed to look like leopard.

DELMAN, 1995   NANCY GIALLOMBARDO, 1990s

André Courrèges, dubbed the "Corbusier of Paris couture" in *Women's Wear Daily*, trained both as an engineer and as a cutter for the great Spanish designer Balenciaga. His Fall '64 collection drew on both parts of his background. Featured in the collection were flared minidresses with plastic portholes for waistlines and an assortment of hats shaped like platters and space helmets. But even more revolutionary was the footwear: low-heeled, calf-high boots made of white plastic and ornamented only with a clear cutout slot near the top. Quickly moving from the

André Courrèges, 1964

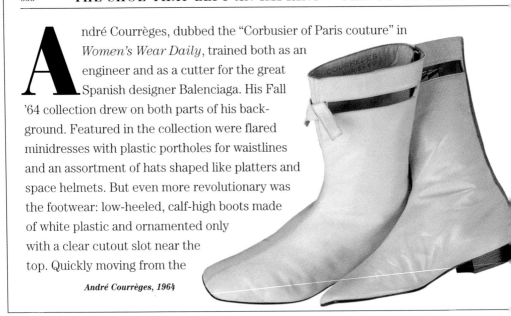

Courrèges-inspired ensemble, 1966

runway to the dance floor, the "Go-go" boot projected a futuristic space-age couture and signaled the end of a fashion world dictated by a handful of Parisian designers.

Boots became the best-selling footwear of the decade and came in a wide range of looks and lengths. They were worn with minis, as a way of dressing up newly revealed legs, and with the pants that more women were wearing as a symbol of liberation. So widely imitated was Courrèges that in 1965 he briefly shuttered his design house. Though he relaunched his business two years later, none of his subsequent designs ever matched the success of his little white boots.

"Cristal" by Roger Vivier, 1966

Thigh-high boots were originally worn by pirates and smugglers, who tucked stolen valuables or "booty" into them—a practice that gave rise to the term "bootlegging."

THESE THIGH-HIGHS, worn by pre-feminist Jane Fonda in the Roger Vadim movie *Barbarella,* are a racy replacement for a garter belt and stockings.

GIULIO COLTELLACCI, 1968

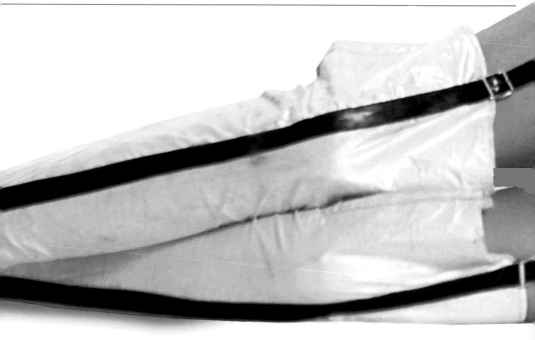

"FLOWER POWER" BOOTS, worn with the ankle-length granny dresses of the early 1970s, seem to epitomize the psychedelic experience.

SAKS FIFTH AVENUE, 1970S

GRANNY TAKES A TRIP, 1970S

A CENTURY AGO, the flower brocade boots that peeked out beneath ankle-length skirts embodied all the elegance of Florentine designs.

ITALIAN, C. 1885

THE 1950S OVERSHOE,
or galosh, covered in
cotton velvet and trimmed
in rabbit fur, is a distant
cousin of the carriage
boot (facing page).

*The foul-weather boot
worn by ancient Romans
was an adaptation of one
worn by the Gauls. Over time,
the Gaulish boot became the
galosh.*

AMERICAN, 1950S

IN COLD WEATHER, elegant quilted boots called "Juliets" were donned for traveling in carriages. Upon arrival, they were slipped off and replaced with an evening shoe.

AMERICAN, C. 1900

WELLINGTONS, those clunky moss-green rubber boots, are typically worn for mucking around the English countryside. Karl Lagerfeld gave the "Wellie" status by changing its color and branding it with the Chanel logo.

KARL LAGERFELD, 1994

VII. STILTED BEHAVIOR: CHOPINES & PLATFORMS

en have been putting women up on pedestals, bewitchingly out of reach, for centuries. And fashion followed suit—at times verging on the ridiculous. In 16th-century Venice, shoes called chopines placed women's feet on platforms that frequently rose to unprecedented heights of 30 inches or more. Made of cork or wood, the platforms themselves were usually upholstered in leather or jeweled velvet to match the shoes they supported.

Derived from a style so popular in 15th-century Spain that it almost exhausted that country's cork supply, the Venetian chopine became a major symbol of social status and great wealth.

This page: a velvet-covered chopine, Venice, c. 1560 (above), and 20-inch wood and leather chopine, Venice, late 15th century (right). Preceding page: Nina, 1970s.

Two servants were required to steady the wearer of such ridiculously impractical shoes, but women wore them proudly—despite the derisive laughter of tourists who flocked to Venice just to see these living statues on their towering pedestals.

The demand for chopines spread to France and England, where women teetered stoically on platforms too high for unassisted expeditions from home. The "walking footstools," as they were known, fell out of fashion two centuries later, once it was discovered that lowering the sole in front made high shoes easier to manage. The heel was born, and red ones replaced chopines as status shoes.

Platforms never again soared as high as the chopine, but they have become fashionable again in this century at roughly 20-year intervals. The first was at the end of the 1930s when the diminutive,

Super-platform, 1970s

turbaned Carmen Miranda landed in Hollywood carrying suitcases full of glittery wedged soles. At that time, European designers were making platform shoes from synthetic materials as a practical solution to the era's shortages of leather and wood. Ferragamo rose to the challenge, layering cork and covering it with waxed canvas, to create some of the most memorable shoes of his career.

Nina's 11-inch display platform, 1970s

Platforms went out of style in the postwar years, but were reintroduced by Vivier in 1967, and became a full-blown fashion statement in the psychedelic '70s. Early in the decade, as bell-bottoms widened, platforms thickened and became more outrageously decorative. Despite doctors' warnings of spine damage from these awkward,

Glittery disco platform, 1970s

clunky shoes, they were worn by both men and women—including pop stars such as Diana Ross, Stevie Nicks and Elton John, who owned a huge collection.

Disco nostalgia spawned another revival in the early 1990s, and club kids madly pounded dance floors in rhinestone-covered platforms and foot-high vinyl sneakers. The GAP offered a more modest 2-inch leather sandal wedge for the less courageous. Though women still fall off them as inelegantly as they did hundreds of years ago, and though they still raise as many eyebrows as they do feet, it's a pretty safe bet that in another 20 years or so the platform will rise again.

A lyrical Lucite sole with floating rose petals, Christian Louboutin, 1996

CEREMONIAL GETAS,
here painted with flying
cranes and chrysanthe-
mums, are worn to temple
by young Japanese girls for
the Shi Chi Gosan coming-
of-age ritual.

JAPANESE, 1950s

CHOPINES were pieced together from stacks of cork and upholstered in rich velvet. The guilloche design on the base of this platform was wrought from silver-gilt filigree and large-headed tacks.

Venetian husbands reputedly introduced heavy wooden chopines to prevent their wives from straying.

VENETIAN, 1600s

PLATFORMS COMPOSED
of layered Sardinian cork
were a practical solution
to the wartime shortage
of wood, steel and leather.
This rainbow sandal
exudes the Hollywood
glitz that inspired many
of Ferragamo's creations.

SALVATORE FERRAGAMO, 1938

CHURCH AUTHORITIES, generally the last to condone extravagant fashions, approved of the chopine because by limiting movement, it discouraged wearers from participating in sinful activities like dancing.

VENETIAN, 16TH CENTURY

VENETIAN, 16TH CENTURY

"Venetian ladies are made of three things: one part wood, meaning the chopines; another part was their apparel and the third part was a woman."
—*visitor to Venice, 17th century*

PERUGIA'S PLATFORM mule was one of the last flamboyant gasps before wartime austerity. The dot-and-circle punchwork patterning of a 15th-century chopine (facing page) derived from bookbinding.

ANDRÉ PERUGIA, 1939

Called "cow hoofs" and "ox muzzles," chopines were ridiculed in their day and ranked among the greatest monstrosities of footwear.

VENETIAN, 1490s

IN THE OTTOMAN
Empire, women wore
stilted sandals to protect
their feet from the dust
of the streets and the
floors of the public baths.
These wooden sandals,
inlaid with mother-of-
pearl, were reserved for
special occasions.

TURKISH OR SYRIAN,
EARLY 20TH CENTURY

ITALIAN, 1600

AN ITALIAN CHOPINE called a *zoccolo* was supported by 7-inch columns that left the arch of the foot floating in midair and made walking a particularly difficult exercise.

In 16th-century England, if a bride falsified her height by wearing chopines, her husband was entitled to an annulment.

AMERICAN, 1940s

SAKS FIFTH AVENUE, 1940s

PLATFORM SLING-backs, considered racy in the 1940s, were made even racier with rows of rhinestones or studs. Posters of Rita Hayworth wearing David Evins satin platforms (near left) were a fixture in many U.S. servicemen's lockers.

DAVID EVINS, 1940s

IN 1936, FERRAGAMO developed his celebrated orthopedic wedge by sculpting two pieces of wood into an "F"-shape. Within two years of its introduction in the U.S., 75 percent of American shoes had some kind of wedge heel.

SALVATORE FERRAGAMO, 1944

THE FLOATING WEDGE, engineered by Dutch designer Jan Jansen, sits far forward on the arch and gives the illusion of a heel-less high heel. Molded of plastic, the wedge cushions the foot.

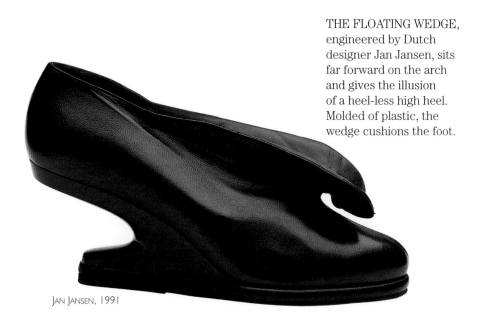

JAN JANSEN, 1991

CARVED AND PAINTED
wooden wedge shoes were
witty tourist souvenirs
sold in the Philippines
after World War II.

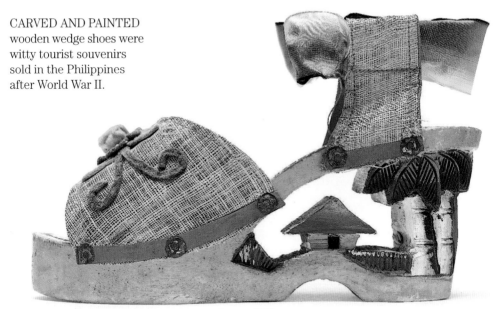

FILIPINO, 1945

EXOTIC MARKINGS
on a lacquered wooden
platform add spice to
the suede-and-straw
upper of a shoe created
in Paris during the
German occupation.

FRENCH, 1943

THE KAPKAP, a tall wooden clog, was once worn by closeted harem beauties. Its name derives from the sound of the stilts hitting marble.

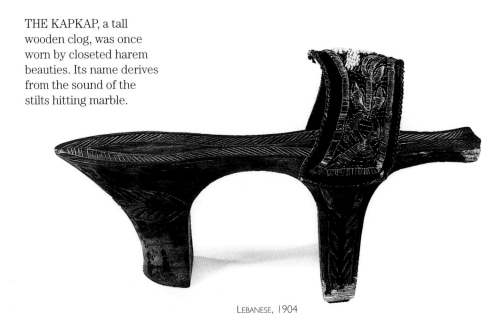

LEBANESE, 1904

THE VIADUCT-STYLE base of Arpad's clog-like creation was engineered with a hinged shank for greater flexibility.

STEVEN ARPAD, 1939

MANCHU WOMEN with unbound feet wore shoes on pedestals to imitate the mincing "Lotus foot" step admired by Chinese men. The stilt-like bases were made from sewn layers of starched cotton.

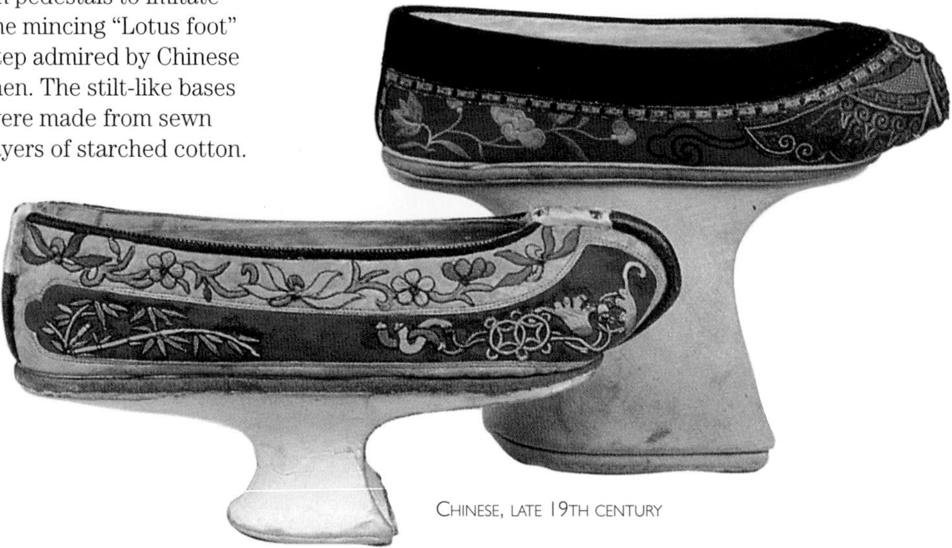

CHINESE, LATE 19TH CENTURY

CHINESE, 1890s

THE NOTCHED SOLE
of the ancient clog sandal
was reinterpreted by
Vivier with a sculptor's
sensibility.

ROGER VIVIER, 1990s

THE RENCHIBA GETA
is a thong clog whose
tooth-like platform is cut
from one piece of wood.
The style was tradition-
ally worn by the Oiran,
the highest class of
Japanese geisha, who
burned their old getas
and stamped the ashes
into the ground with the
new pair.

*Emperor Hirohito
of Japan stood on
12-inch-high getas for his
1926 coronation.*

JAPANESE, 1984

S
alvatore Ferragamo, whose name is synonymous with superb Italian craftsmanship, made his first pair of shoes at age nine. His parents, poor farmers in the tiny village of Bonito, couldn't afford to buy shoes for his sisters, who were about to celebrate their first communion. Faced with the shame of seeing them wear clogs to church, Salvatore borrowed materials

Ferragamo inspects the sole of a design, 1952.

from the local cobbler and made the shoes himself. At age 14, after studying shoemaking in nearby Naples, he opened a shop in his parents' home, where he supervised six assistants as they hand-sewed women's shoes that had more verve than anything else crafted in the Neapolitan region.

Pure ambition brought him to the States at age 16 and then to Hollywood; directors such as DeMille and Griffith featured his cowboy boots, Roman sandals and moccasins in their silent movies. Swanson, Dietrich, Pickford and Garbo flocked to his Hollywood Boulevard store, buying custom-made designs that bristled with wit, originality and opulence. Ferragamo improvised with unorthodox materials, "here a Spanish shawl, there a Chinese brocade or a yard of Indian silk or a chair with a petit point back." He made shoes from hummingbird feathers and tree bark, carved prow-shaped toes that resembled suede parrot beaks, fashioned

Facing page: dramatic, statuesque platform fashioned for the stage, 1938. Right: the first "orthopedic" wedge, 1935.

1944 sandal with hemp vamp, Oriental toe and fluted layers of upholstered cork

heels to look like corkscrews and, after the discovery of King Tut's tomb, inverted pyramids.

But his thriving reputation as "Shoemaker to the Stars" only partially satisfied him. He could not fathom why his shoes pleased the eye yet hurt the foot, so he proceeded to study anatomy at the University of Southern California and learned that the weight of the body falls onto the arch of the foot. After some experimentation, he perfected a steel arch support that he inserted into the instep of every shoe. For the first time in history, women's shoes were both stylish and comfortable.

Ferragamo returned home in 1927 and planted the seeds for what would become one of Italy's largest fashion dynasties. He set up shop in Florence, and

1942 wedge with suede patchwork upper

hired expert craftsmen to carve lasts as well as skilled *montatores* to position the uppers by hand. Technical expertise was the heart of his business and preceded his entry into the world of fashion.

His most famous invention was probably the cork wedge, which paved the way for the inspired platform shoes he fashioned during the war. Throughout the 1940s and '50s, his styles—from a cage-shaped brass heel to wedge-shaped suede mules—filled the pages of the world's top fashion magazines. When Ferragamo died in 1960, he left behind 350 patents and a reputation as the man who revolutionized the modern shoe business. "I am very happy to have made the humble trade of shoemaker respectable," he wrote in his autobiography, *Shoemaker of Dreams*. This from the man whose achievements are what gave cachet to the label "Made in Italy."

Velvet and gold-caged pump, 1955

DELMAN'S COMICAL clog with cutout portholes is a takeoff on the Eastern geta.

NINA, 1940

A FUR-TRIMMED CAP protects the toe of this Japanese geta, but the placement of its 3-inch stilts sabotages balance.

JAPANESE, 1980

A PLATFORM SOLE lessens the incline and therefore the discomfort of a high heel. This ankle-strap revival of the platform shoe was perfect for the sharp twists and turns of disco dancing.

AMERICAN,
1970

A PLATFORM WEDGE, unusual on a Lotus shoe, made walking even more of an ordeal for a woman with bound feet.

CHINESE, EARLY 20TH CENTURY

HENRY BEHAR created a line of outrageous rocking platforms in his basement on New York's Lower East Side and called them Goody Two Shoes. This wooden version was inspired by a Life Savers mint.

GOODY TWO
SHOES, 1970s

CHOPINES were outlawed after a scandalous number of pregnant Venetian women fell off them and suffered miscarriages. Nevertheless the fashion was worn throughout Europe and remained popular until the 1800s.

VENETIAN, 1600s

"Your ladyship is nearer to heaven than when I saw you last, by the altitude of the chopine."
—*Shakespeare*

SO-CALLED "WOODEN" platforms from the 1940s were often fabricated from plastic. Lauren's heavy-soled suede shoe, created in the '80s, was the real thing.

RALPH LAUREN, 1980s

HEAVY-DUTY wooden platform pumps created by Japanese designer Rei Kawakubo for Comme des Garçons resemble the sabot, a wooden clog with a slightly turned-up toe.

COMME DES GARÇONS, 1990s

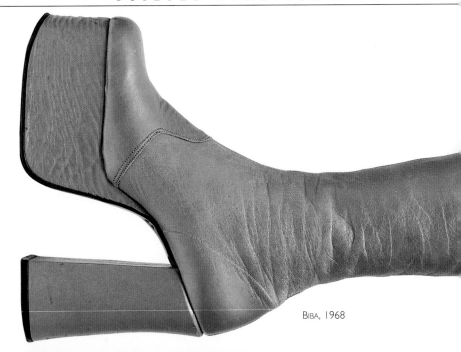

BIBA, 1968

THE SKINTIGHT leather platform boot with a 5-inch heel was designed by Barbara Hulanicki for Biba, the London boutique and clothing line that put '70s British fashion on the world map. Women formed queues in order to purchase it and snapped up 75,000 pairs within a few months.

I n the 1970s, a well-worn Kork-Ease was a very personal thing. Straight from the store, the platform sandals were the color of pale flesh and as conspicuously new as a mint pair of Levis. After about two weeks, however, the neutral suede took on a rich, dark patina, and body weight and heat "molded" the insole to the foot, taking on the wearer's imprint.

While other platforms of the decade were overdecorated and wacky, rising to 6-inch heights, Kork-Ease was the staple, no-nonsense version—the one sported by every groovy dresser. It combined the cushioned softness of the earthbound Birkenstock with a modishly high wedge.

Julius and Sol Stern marketed Kork-Ease out of a small office on New York's Canal Street, and they

Kork-Ease,
early 1970s

had to ration sales because the demand was so great. "Nobody actually designed them," recalls their chief salesman, Sam Hersh. "We told the factory what we wanted, and they made them!"

Kork-Ease were affordable—between $25 and $40 a pair. Their signature crisscross vamp was made from vegetable-tanned water buffalo hide and their cork wedges were so comfortable, says Hersh, that "you could have worn them to bed!" Intended primarily for women, they were bought by both sexes and prized for their lightness.

MIA, 1993

Fashion designer Betsey Johnson, who remembers them as a "Greenwich Village thing," owned at least 10 pairs, including the originals and flashy copies in cobalt blue, silver lamé and gold glitter. "After the low, chunky shoes of the '60s," she says, "we needed something outrageous and funky."

In the mid '90s, orthopedic-looking platforms again became stylish, and the Kork-Ease sandal was re-created by a number of companies.

"1972: The first woman falls off her cork sandals. Millions follow."   —*Vogue*

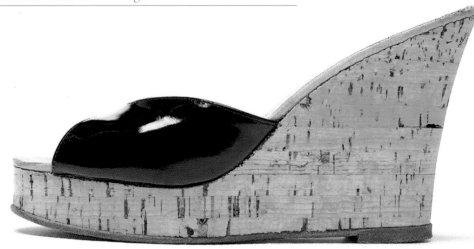

DELMAN, 1970s

CORK'S LIGHTWEIGHT properties have always made it ideal for platforms. Tough and weather-resistant, it also molds easily to the contours of the foot.

VICTORIA PRATT, 1990s

In 1955, Carmen Miranda, the 5-foot Brazilian bombshell who performed atop 8-inch platforms, recorded a hit song entitled "I Like to Be Tall."

AMERICAN, 1980s

AMERICAN, 1970s

MOST PLATFORMS don't take themselves too seriously. Two cases in point: rainbow-colored stacked rubber flip-flops (facing page) and a 6-inch-high carved wooden clog with a tiki head and AstroTurf vamp.

"You put me high upon a pedestal. So high that I could almost see eternity. You needed me." —*Randy Goodrum, 1978*

AMERICAN, 1970s

AMERICAN, 1970s

HIGH-PLATFORM performers like David Bowie, the King of Glam Rock, brought style and glitter into the streets and onto the feet of both men and women.

IN A CARTOON from the '70s, a woman wearing exceptionally high platform shoes is about to be arrested. "If you come any closer," she yells at the policeman, "I'll jump!"

AMERICAN, 1970s

FOR A '90S LOOK
in platforms, English
designers Nicky Lawler
and Lori Duffy teamed up
to design wedge sandals
with denim uppers.

LAWLER DUFFY, 1994

JOUNY'S "TRAPPER"
combines a Timberland
boot and a high-top
sneaker. Attaching a high
heel and platform to
sneakers is a fad peculiar
to the '90s.

CYD JOUNY, 1994

DUTCH DESIGNER
Jan Jansen intends his
shoes to be "visually
irritating." His hard-
edged, patent-leather
platform resembles
a piece of polished
machinery.

JAN JANSEN, 1996

GAULTIER, the French designer who takes his inspiration as much from the streets as from the theater, put his own spin on the ancient gladiator sandal.

JEAN-PAUL GAULTIER, 1990s

VIII. SHOES OF SCANDAL:
FETISH & LOTUS SHOES

Despite the cultural differences that spawned them, Western fetish shoes and the diminutive Lotus shoes of China both objectify the wearer and whet the sexual appetite of the beholder. But while Western fetishists are more interested in being dominated, in China passivity, symbolized by bound feet, is the key to erotic bliss. Shoe historian Mary Trasko sums up the differences by noting that fetish footwear in the West has always been "slick, hard-edged and weapon-like," while in the East "it reminds one more of lingerie, with satin uppers and delicately embroidered soles."

Western shoe lovers date back to ancient times, but fetishism came into its own and was first given a name in 19th-century England. Victorian repression and prudery

Patent leather fetish pump with 7-inch red heel.
Preceding page: Northern Chinese shoe, 1860s.

generated new outlets for sexual expression. The campaign to conceal the female leg under floor-length skirts and boots was so successful that the mere glimpse of a woman's ankle was cause for arousal. Women's ankles, and by extension their shoes or boots, became symbols of more hidden body parts, and lusting after their feet or footwear was deemed strictly taboo. Not surprisingly, by the 1850s an underground market for pornography and shoes with 6-inch heels flourished in London.

Well over a century later, despite the prevalence of magazines with names like *High Heel Honeys* and *Super Spikes*, shoe fetishism is still taboo, partly because of its association with cross-dressing and S&M. The classic Western fetishist favors shiny black patent leather (for a "wet" look), an extreme version of spike heels (associated with sexually aggressive women) or thigh-high laced boots (worn by statuesque comic book heroines whose torpedo-shaped breasts pop out of scanty latex uniforms). The

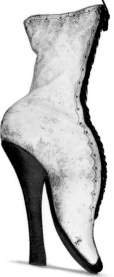

English "Exhibition boot," 1889

high heels inhibit movement—a form of female bondage some find erotic—while their weapon-like shape excites the passive male who revels in being threatened.

But fetishists have individual proclivities. Some shoes, adorned with padlocks, straps and buckled ankle harnesses, suggest subjugation as much as they do dominance and present the foot, according to fashion historian Anne Hollander, as a beautiful slave. In extreme cases, the woman is dispensed with entirely and the fetishist is content to spend his Saturday night dating a high-heeled pump.

Restriction, actual or illusory, seems key in the ability of fetish shoes to excite, no matter the cultural environment. But whereas the height of a shoe connotes eroticism in the West, size is prized in China. Very small feet had been admired by Chinese society long before footbinding took on many of the marks of a cultural

Michel Perry,
1995

Silk embroidered Lotus boot, 1860s

quasi-fetishism. In the 10th century, according to social historians, exotic dancers at the Imperial court wore tight socks to make their feet appear smaller. The custom spread throughout the upper classes and footbinding became a more torturous procedure, as well as a rite of passage. A highborn mother would use astrology to determine the time and date of her daughter's *gin lien* initiation, which would take place between the ages of 3 and 8. After giving the child a pedicure, she would bend the four toes back over the arch and bandage them in place. (The big toe was left free to form a half-moon shape.) After each bathing, the foot was bandaged tighter and then forced into a shoe one size smaller. The hope was to create a cultural rarity: a "Golden Lotus," a foot measuring

Drawing of an adult's 3-inch Lotus foot

three inches. The only time the girl would see her feet uncovered from then on was when they were bathed or, later, if her husband unwrapped the bandages during sexual foreplay.

Despite their misshapen appearance, Lotus feet were looked upon as the most erotic part of a woman's body, and the delicate slippers or bootees worn to cover them were no less delectable. Chinese husbands respectfully coveted their wives' tiny Lotus shoes and would sometimes display them on a small plate (with room to spare) to show off the foot size. Women commonly owned several hundred pairs of these shoes, which varied by region and the fashion of the day, and they spent long hours embroidering them with symbols of fertility, longevity, harmony and union. Shoes worn

Two pairs of 20th-century Lotus shoes

on the wedding night often depicted explicit erotic scenes as a way of instructing the virgin bride.

Footbinding fell out of favor when China became a republic in 1912 and had virtually disappeared in most provinces when Mao officially banned it in 1949. Openly practiced for a thousand years, the ritual is now a source of shame, and Lotus shoes have become collectible relics of a custom the Chinese are anxious to forget.

Ironically, in the West, where fetishism was always considered subversive, a shift in sexual attitudes has given rise to fetish chic. In the last two decades, fetish gear has become not only acceptable but its footwear has been integrated into mainstream fashion.

Elsé Anita, 1996

A DEEP-THROATED shoe, conjuring up the unabashed décolletage of a plunging neckline, flatters the distended curve of a woman's instep. Its 8-inch heel renders the wearer immobile and thrusts the foot forward like an offering.

AUSTRIAN, 19TH CENTURY

PERUGIA designed this fetish pump for the legendary Parisian music-hall star, Mistinguett, who literally went to great heights to greet gentleman callers at the door. Perugia once said, "Every woman is not only conscious of her feet, but sex-conscious of them."

ANDRÉ PERUGIA, 1948

ANKLE HARDWARE in shoe fetish language can be code for either bondage or willing enslavement. It also implies that the wearer considers herself a prize, worthy of being kept under lock and key.

THE LITTLE SHOE BOX, 1996

"High heels are pride and privilege, the passkey to decadence."
—*Karen Heller*

THE LITTLE SHOE BOX, 1996

THE LITTLE SHOE BOX, 1990s

"Within the fetishist subculture, shoes were second only to corsets in popularity."
—*Valerie Steele*

ENGLISH, 1890s

TIGHT LACING excites desire not only because of its restraining effect but also because of its promise of release. These extreme "ballet," or "tip-toe," boots are not intended for walking; rather, they are costumes that set the stage for elaborate role-playing.

A FETISH TOOL,
this kid boot constricts the
woman's leg behind 30
buttons and contorts her
foot by forcing her
instep over her toes.
The 11-inch heel
incapacitates the wearer
but also supplies her
with a formidable weapon.

AUSTRIAN, 1900s

A COMMON ASSUMPTION is that fetishists like to be trampled on. Not so. Some like to be ridden by women wearing boots or shoes with spurs.

EUROPEAN, C. 1890

THIERRY MUGLER, 1991

EXAGGERATED
platforms elevate the
wearer to goddess status
and create a distance
from reality that ignites
forbidden fantasies.

ENGLISH, 1970s

BRAZILIAN,
1980s

PARTLY OBSCURED here by leather cross-hatching (near right) and a ladder of barrettes, the ankle and foot become tantalizing.

EUROPEAN, 1938

SWISS, 1916

LOUBOUTIN'S VELVET
pump drapes the ankle
with net and tassels
inspired by a belly
dancer's veil.

CHRISTIAN
LOUBOUTIN, 1990

FETISH SHOES, impervious to fashion trends, never go out of style.

ELSÉ ANITA, 1996

BAWDY, BUXOM actress Mae West was top box-office news in the 1930s. She accentuated her hourglass figure and invented her hip-circling sway to balance on these 8-inch-high platforms, adding new dimension to her catchphrase, "Come up and see me sometime."

AMERICAN, 1930s

"Goddesses live in the heavens. They do not stand, they do not walk, they glide and sway. The goddesses are laughing and balance on heels as slender as the tip of a little finger."—*Lola Pagola*

AUSTRIAN,
1935

THE FETISH LOOK
has been appropriated
by fashion. Even the ven-
erable house of Chanel
issued fetish versions of its
classic two-toned pump.

CHANEL, 1990s

Vivienne Westwood, Britain's *grande dame terrible* of fashion, lives by two mottoes: "If it's conservative, it's dead," and "When in doubt, overdress." In the early '70s, two decades before designers Gaultier, Mugler and Alaïa came up with the notion of fetish streetwear, Westwood

Classic pump with concealed platform, 1995

was parading around London decked out in stiletto heels, rubber hosiery and negligés. She and her former partner, Malcolm McLaren, emerged from that anarchistic period as the creators of Punk fashion. "It all came from an irritation with orthodox ways of dressing and a

This 8-inch staggerer (1994) tripped up a runway model.

Westwood in 1996: prim and proper, at least from the waist up

certain perversity," she says in retrospect.

Her collections continue to be influenced by fetish gear—some were named Witches, Cut, Slash and Pull, Pagan and Savage—but even the see-through dresses she wears on British television or to a royal reception can't upstage her outrageous shoes and boots.

Primarily a clothing designer, Westwood got into

Funky chic: the "Elevated Court," 1994

shoes because she couldn't find any outlandish enough for her ensembles. For the last decade she and her collaborator Murray Blewett have concocted a whole repertoire of shocking footwear, including the infamous lace-ups that felled veteran

"Golf Satyr," 1995

model Naomi Campbell on the runway. Like her clothing, Westwood's footwear parodies the shape of the body. In her usual straightforward manner, she justifies the impracticality of her designs as a way to rally against the bourgeois. "Slightly uncomfortable footwear," she says, "exaggerates the posture and forces people to question how they walk."

Patent leather stiletto boots, 1994

Today the black sheep of fashion has become almost respectable. She's been hailed by *Women's Wear Daily* as one of the most influential designers in the world. And her London boutique is patronized these days by a loyal bevy of aristocratic aficionados who get a kick out of her over-the-top aesthetic and shrug off the notion that her shoes are degenerate and unwearable.

Like Westwood herself, they find most fashion mediocre and banal, and they appreciate the irony of designs that juxtapose the traditional and the taboo.

An exaggerated D'Orsay pump, called "Satyr" because of its hoof-like heel, 1995. Above, shoe from "On Liberty" collection, 1994.

FUR AND SUEDE are like
cake and ice cream to a
shoe fetishist. Westwood's
father-in-law, an iron-
monger, sculpted the
8-inch prototype heel for
these fetish boots from a
piece of brass plumbing.
Originally intended solely
for the runway, more than
300 pairs have been sold
through Westwood's
London boutique.

"I like to literally put women on a pedestal."—*Vivienne Westwood*

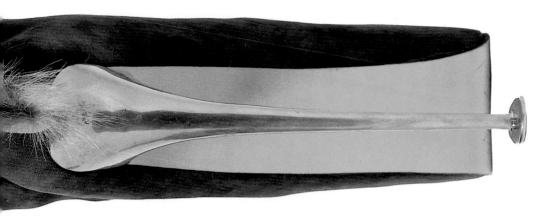

VIVIENNE WESTWOOD, 1995

A ROUNDED BACKSIDE balances the hourglass curves of Bally's turn-of-the-century black pump. Ferragamo's "prow toe" (facing page) recalls the phallic poulaine favored by medieval courtiers.

BALLY, 1890s

SALVATORE FERRAGAMO,
1930s

SKINTIGHT BOOTS accentuate the curve of a leg as a tight skirt accentuates the hips. Because boots are actually men's footwear appropriated by women, they carry ambiguous, gender-crossing overtones and trigger an erotic charge.

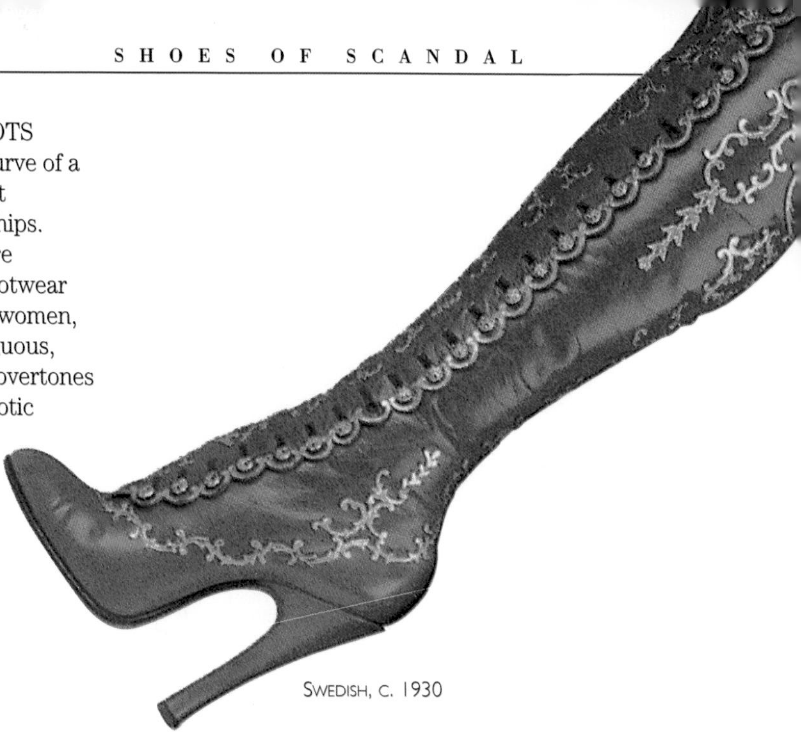

SWEDISH, C. 1930

MANOLO BLAHNIK,
1990s

"Desire, which beleaguers all
men, has a special foolscap for
the shoe fetishist. He may find
himself baying softly at the
windows of some high-end
shoe boutique. . . . " —*Chip Brown*

CLASSIC BONDAGE
inspired the design
of this strapped rhine-
stone pedestal boot from
Hellstern intended to
both elevate the wearer
and hobble her walk. The
legendary Parisian bottier
produced some of the
most luxurious fetish
footwear of the Roaring
Twenties.

HELLSTERN & SONS, 1920s

BLACK IS THE COLOR
of Western fetishism, but
red is strong in both West
and East. The lattice
overlay on this knee-high
kid boot extends the
bondage theme.

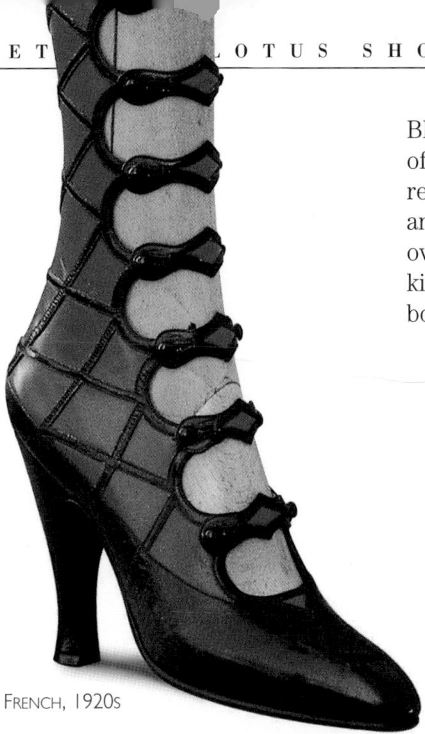

FRENCH, 1920s

THE PUNK STYLE of
leather and studs crossed
over from political statement to high-fashion fetish
with this pump from Yves
Saint Laurent. A boot that
closes with 30 buttons
enticingly prolongs the
art of dressing—and
undressing—the foot.

YVES SAINT LAURENT,
C. 1985

SWEDISH, C. 1925

VITTORIO RICCI, 1993

RAZOR-SHARP TOES
(facing page) and a
jagged, knife-like heel
carry all the delicious
danger of a lethal dagger.

ENGLISH, 1993

CYD JOUNY, 1990s

AN ERECT ANKLE and extended leg is the biological sign of sexual availability in several animal species. Both spike heels and the Lotus shoe (facing page) force the leg into what anthropologists call a "courtship strut."

AMERICAN, 1990s

"Perhaps women were once so dangerous they had to have their feet bound."
—*Maxine Hong Kingston*

Chinese, c. 1890s

A DAINTY CUP was often placed in the heel pocket of a Lotus shoe and incorporated into male drinking rituals.

CHINESE,
LATE 19TH CENTURY

A GOLDEN LOTUS, a foot no longer than three inches, was the cultural ideal. This shoe belonged to a woman with Silver Lotuses, feet measuring 4 inches.

CHINESE,
1900

actual size, 4"

Northern Chinese, 1880-90

A BUTTERFLY, centered above the heel on a spring, fluttered and trembled whenever the wearer (or lover) moved her minuscule bound foot. This extremely rare pair of Silver Lotuses (side view on facing page) probably titillated the clients of a Chinese prostitute.

NORTHERN CHINESE, 1880-90

EACH LOTUS SHOE
encoded meaning in its
use of color and embroi-
dered figures. The peony
motif on this red shoe
indicates it was worn in
springtime. The color
black on the Shanghai-
style shoes (facing page)
suggests they were worn
by an older woman.

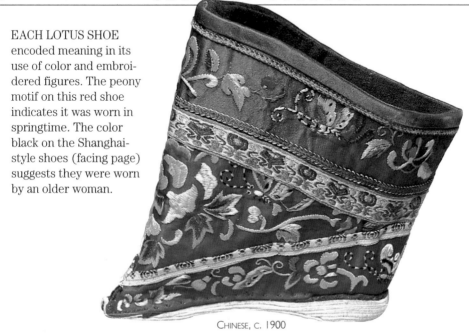

CHINESE, C. 1900

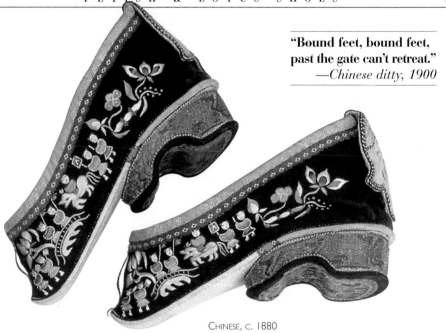

**"Bound feet, bound feet,
past the gate can't retreat."**
—*Chinese ditty, 1900*

CHINESE, C. 1880

ORNATE UNDERSOLES
of shoes worn by women
who spent many hours
reclining were conspicu-
ous placards of leisure
and wealth. These soles
feature loose leather flaps
for a husband to play
with.

CHINESE, 19TH CENTURY

As standard foreplay, a Chinese husband would gently remove his wife's shoes and unswathe her feet. The bandages, 10-foot-long strips of cotton or silk, sometimes held wives secure in acts of bondage.

CHINESE,
19TH CENTURY

A FASHIONABLE STYLE for foreplay, this shoe was constructed with a throat known as the "Temple Gate" and lacings called "Ladder Rungs." Lotus shoes for bed, often depicting erotic scenes, wore out more quickly than those for daytime wear.

CHINESE,
EARLY 20TH CENTURY

IX. ART & SOLE: ONE-OF-A-KIND SHOES

Unique in conception and execution, shoes that take flight from a designer's fantasies become dreams realized on the foot, elevating the shoe to a work of art. It is no coincidence that Salvatore Ferragamo, who devoted his life to fashioning the perfect shoe, thought of himself as a "shoemaker of dreams." "There is no limit to beauty, no saturation point in design," he mused in his autobiography, "no end to the materials a shoemaker may use to decorate his creations."

Fabricated of every conceivable material, one-of-a-kind footwear ranges from the eccentric and extravagant to the witty and iconoclastic, making use of everything from pearls and medieval textiles, feathers and fish scales, to AstroTurf and postage stamps.

Some designs are feats of technical daring, a

Say it in spades—bold graphics from a student designer, 1996.
Preceding page: André Perugia's "Homage to Picasso," 1950.

Anna de Logardière's costume shoe, 1994

defiance of gravity to resolve the shoemaker's greatest challenge—a shoe with no visible means of support, the "heel-less heel." Or, in Beth Levine's case, a "Topless" mule.

Perhaps the most renowned one-of-a-kind shoes are those created specifically for movies. Such designs are shaped by the need to convey a personality or mood, or to build a character from the ground up. Certainly the most famous pair of movie shoes—perhaps the most famous pair of shoes in all the world—are the sparkling ruby slippers worn in 1939 by Judy Garland in *The Wizard of Oz*. As she skipped along the Yellow Brick Road to adventure and new horizons, their magic was—and still is—truly one of a kind.

Nancy Giallombardo's Pekingese mule, 1994

WINGS, LIKE SHOES, have always been metaphors for mobility, speed and grace. Here, the mythical bird Hintha roosts on the vamp of a sequined slipper that once adorned the feet of Burmese royalty.

BURMESE, LATE 1800s

AN ARTIST'S rendering
of the expression "with
wings on one's feet,"
Calonaci's golden pump
pays homage to Mercury,
the wing-sandaled
messenger of the gods.

GIUSEPPE CALONACI,
1992

HIGHLY POLISHED cabochon "emeralds" and a galaxy of twinkling rhinestones pave the silk surface of this pump, created in 1961 for Ava Gardner.

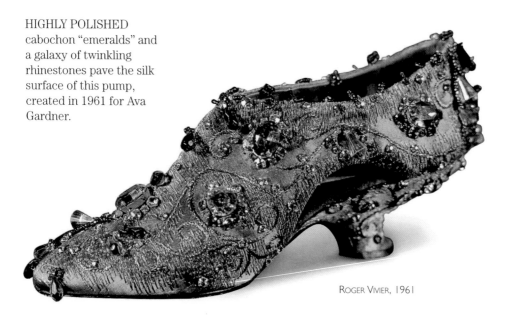

ROGER VIVIER, 1961

A PRECIOUS CARGO of 18-karat gold chain necklaces, anchored by miniature bells, adorns Ferragamo's showstopping sandal, which sold for $1,000 a pair—an unheard-of price in the 1950s.

SALVATORE FERRAGAMO, 1956

André Perugia, 1937

Jan Jansen, 1994

TROMPE L'OEIL shoes create the illusion that the wearer is suspended in midair. Perugia was the first to experiment with a heel-less heel (far left). Jansen's technical feat of balance resolved, in his words, "an unsettling point of tension." The sole of Pinet's sleek gold and suede pump tapers off into a steel-plate support.

FRANÇOIS PINET, 1950s

MOVIE MILESTONES: these sequined red pumps, worn by Judy Garland's Dorothy in the 1939 classic film, transported her to the magical world of Oz. In 1988, an anonymous fan paid $165,000 for them at auction.

ADRIAN, 1939

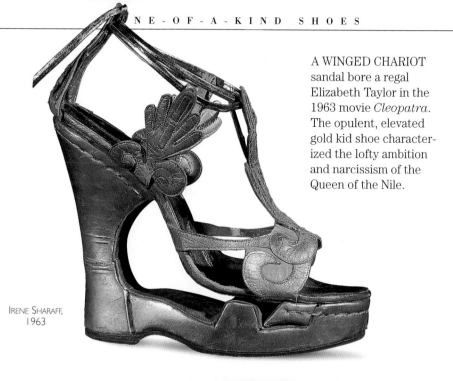

A WINGED CHARIOT sandal bore a regal Elizabeth Taylor in the 1963 movie *Cleopatra*. The opulent, elevated gold kid shoe characterized the lofty ambition and narcissism of the Queen of the Nile.

IRENE SHARAFF,
1963

CINDERELLA'S revenge,
a glass slipper that transforms a charmaid into
a princess, has spawned
playful interpretations
by many contemporary
artists. Lars Hagen's
cut-glass and mirror
collage connotes the
vanity and pain
inherent in the too-
small shoe.

Lars Hagen, 1991

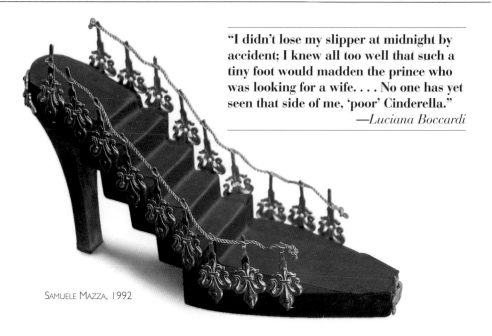

"I didn't lose my slipper at midnight by accident; I knew all too well that such a tiny foot would madden the prince who was looking for a wife. . . . No one has yet seen that side of me, 'poor' Cinderella."
—*Luciana Boccardi*

SAMUELE MAZZA, 1992

NICOLETTI PERCHED latticed leather bootlets atop silver scaffolds, creating double-entendre footwear for Joan of Arc in a 1989 operatic production.

ODETTE NICOLETTI, 1989

THIS GOLD LAMÉ pedestal shoe, bordered with pearls and overlaid with iconic metal dragons, was a one-of-a-kind historic re-creation for Joan Chen's role in *The Last Emperor*. Opulent authentic period costumes earned an Academy Award for designer James Acheson.

JAMES ACHESON, 1987

RICHLY ROMANTIC, Yantorny's designs often combined rare antique laces with Renaissance textiles. A perfectionist of the highest order, he catered to an elite clientele who frequently waited two years for a custom design from his Paris atelier.

"A shoe without sex appeal is as barren as a tree without leaves."—*Rita de Acosta Lydig, Yantorny patron*

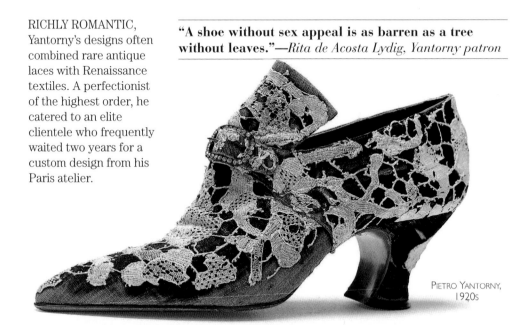

PIETRO YANTORNY,
1920s

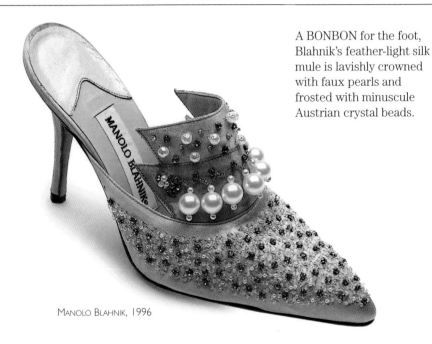

A BONBON for the foot, Blahnik's feather-light silk mule is lavishly crowned with faux pearls and frosted with minuscule Austrian crystal beads.

MANOLO BLAHNIK, 1996

ISRAELI-BORN ARTIST
Levine conceived this
fantasy pump to show-
case a treasure trove of
tiny antique glass beads.
Each bead was laboriously
hand-knotted on strings,
which were then attached
to a wire frame skeleton.

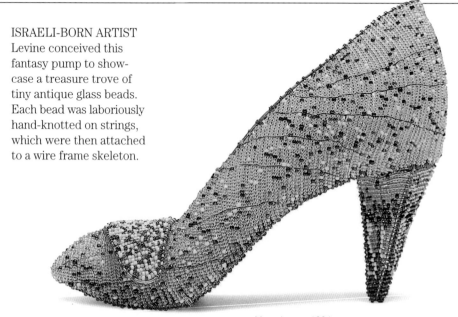

YONA LEVINE, 1984

THE ROMANTIC beauty
of a lace remnant from
an old dress too lovely
to discard inspired Levine
to cobble this keepsake
high heel. Feminine and
mysterious, it hints at a
glamorous, party-filled
past.

YONA LEVINE, 1984

MOVIE SHOE MOMENT:
Anita Ekberg casts aside
these extravagant satin
stilettos to frolic in the
Trevi fountain in *La Dolce
Vita*. Her seductive
wardrobe helped to
portray Fellini's vision of
a shallow and decadent
Roman society.

PIERO GHERARDI, 1960

LOUBOUTIN designed this provocative prototype of the "Egg" pump to focus attention on what he feels is the most sensual, yet ignored part of a woman's foot—the inside curve of the arch.

CHRISTIAN LOUBOUTIN, 1988

BETH LEVINE devised spare, aerodynamically daring "Kabuki" pumps to give the illusion of flight, allowing the wearer to feel as if she were walking on air. Their jet-stream defiance of space prompted Levine to observe in retrospect, "I should have called them 'Airplane' pumps."

BETH LEVINE, 1964

"The history of footwear is one of endless conceits and fantasies."—*Colin McDowell*

BETH LEVINE, 1964

S howcased in museums these days, rather than in fashionable stores, Beth Levine's shoes have lost none of their revolutionary flair.

Spring-O-lator mule, 1952

Levine worked in both journalism and advertising before her size 4B feet landed her a job as a shoe model at Palter-DeLiso, the firm that outraged a prudish public in the late '30s by selling open-toed day pumps. But she had bigger dreams—literally. "I knew I wanted to get into product design," she recalls, "and at night I'd have dreams about making shoes." She married businessman Herbert Levine in 1944, and two years later they started their own shoe company: "Herb handled the business, and I thought up outrageous things to keep him amused."

Witty race car loafer, 1966

Halston and other trend-setters

Beth Levine in her 6th Avenue showroom, 1970

were among the clients who regularly dropped by her Manhattan studio, as were Babe Paley, Bette Davis and Barbra Streisand. When Liza Minnelli needed a pair of untraditional wedding shoes, she turned to Levine and came away with a pair of red sequined pumps. When Nancy Sinatra wanted boots made for walking, it was Levine who created them.

"Cubist" pump, 1967

She had no formal training ("I still can't make a shoe, but I can tell someone how to do it with my eyes closed") but managed to lure the industry's top craftsmen to work for her, hand-carving lasts and perfectly matching the exotic skins she was known to use.

An uncanny knack for predicting trends, a healthy appreciation of the ironic and a dead-sure aesthetic sense allowed Levine to launch one daring design after another. She was the first to mass-produce rhinestone pavé pumps, and she

Minnelli's "ruby slipper," 1967

pioneered both the shoe stocking and the stretch vinyl boot in the early '50s—a full decade before the rest of the world discovered the style. She fashioned heels from woods typically used in the construction of furniture, including beech and mahogany. She streamlined the silhouette of the clear vinyl pump by attaching its transparent Lucite heel without nails. And she constantly experimented with materials—Ultrasuede,

A vinyl take on the glass slipper, 1963

AstroTurf and animal hides like frog skin. She braided play money into a sandal vamp and carved a teakwood salad bowl into a "rock-a-bottom" sole.

To create her "Topless" shoe, one of her most playful conceits, she covered a cushioned sole with red satin and, at the points where the heel and ball of the foot touched the insole, installed pads soaked in spirit gum. The pads stuck to the sole of the foot, and the heel appeared to be an extension of the wearer's heel. "It worked!" says Levine. "We even have movies of a woman dancing in a pair."

Though she retired from the business in 1976, shoes still dance through her dreams. "Recently," she says, "I had a nightmare that some-one had created a fantastic line of ingeniously original shoes, each one better than the next, and boy, was I jealous. When I woke up, I calmed down. I realized that I was the designer!"

Bare-boned "Topless" shoe, 1959

A BED OF NAILS: these sandals were worn by devout Hindus on special pilgrimages to fulfill a vow to the gods for a favor bestowed.

INDIAN, 19TH CENTURY

FLOWER POWER flourishes on Levine's "Splendor in the Grass" sandals with AstroTurf soles and a plastic dahlia embellishment. The playful use of novel materials was a hallmark of Levine's designs.

BETH LEVINE, 1967

NICOLETTI'S pairing of masculine toes with feminine bow ties resulted in these androgynous gold kid and grosgrain platform shoes, designed for a production of Mozart's *Idomeneo* at La Scala.

ODETTE NICOLETTI, 1990

"Nothing has been invented yet that will do a better job than heels at making a good pair of legs look great, or great ones look fabulous." —*Stuart Weitzman*

WEITZMAN preserved his first shoe design for posterity by dipping it in bronze like a baby's shoe.

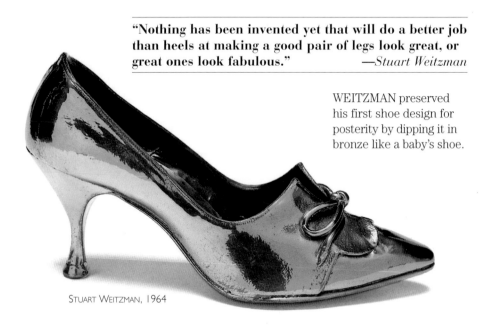

STUART WEITZMAN, 1964

"It's impossible not to smile when you wear a pair of my shoes."
—*Andrea Pfister*

THIS HALF-BOOT was a tongue-in-cheek salute to the great vaudeville singer Al Jolson.

ANDREA PFISTER, 1979

AN ODE to industry, Perugia's pump celebrates the Machine Age with a "rosette" gear and a heel of twisted steel.

ANDRÉ PERUGIA, 1950

WESTWOOD created a
pump with a suede draw-
string "shoebag" upper
for her mud-colored "Buf-
falo Girls" collection.

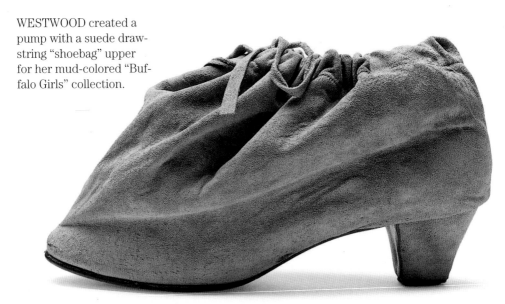

VIVIENNE WESTWOOD, 1983

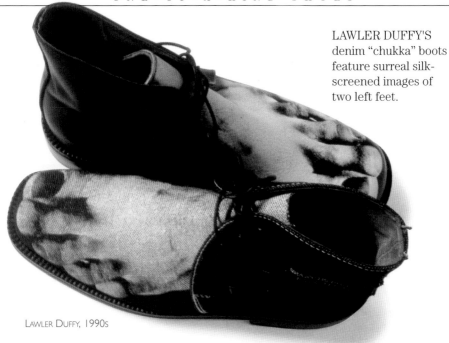

LAWLER DUFFY'S denim "chukka" boots feature surreal silk-screened images of two left feet.

LAWLER DUFFY, 1990s

LYRICAL CURLICUES
covering this pixie boot
exemplify the calligraphic
"trapunto" leather
embossing technique
invented by Arpad.

STEVEN ARPAD, 1930s

A SUNNY PARIS day inspired Giallombardo to remove her straw chapeau, reblock it and contour this mule with sinuous folds and crevices.

NANCY GIALLOMBARDO, 1990

THIS EXTRAVAGANTLY plumed work by Marina Dempster blurs the line between sculpture and shoe. Using a technique inspired by the pre-Columbian Huichol art of "transformational yarn painting," the artist embeds embroidery thread and glass beads into a layer of beeswax and resin.

MARINA DEMPSTER, 2008

THESE SEQUINED platforms were custom-made by bad boy designers Dolce & Gabbana for the sometimes bad girl Madonna.

DOLCE & GABBANA, 1990S

PERUGIA'S PISCINE
pump of overlaid kid
with decorative "scales"
is a tribute to Georges
Braque, the French
Cubist artist.

ANDRÉ PERUGIA,
1931

"BOTANIC COUTURE" is the ephemeral result when Danish still-life photographer Heilmann transforms vegetables and flowers into fantasy footwear. Here, every part of the lowly leek was used to craft this bulb-toed pump.

STINE HEILMANN,
1996

BENES CREATED this shoe, using a papier–mâché technique, from part of a $6 million cache of shredded bills he obtained from the Federal Reserve Board.

BARTON LIDICE BENES,
1984

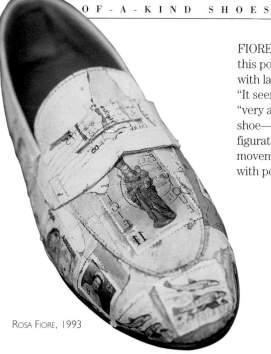

FIORE COLLAGED
this postal penny loafer
with layered envelopes.
"It seemed," she says,
"very apt to make a
shoe—which literally and
figuratively symbolizes
movement and travel—
with postage stamps."

ROSA FIORE, 1993

SHIMIZU, a student at Studio Berçot in Paris, fashioned this "Chaussure de Poisson" by embedding snippets of leather and paillettes into a clay fish sculpture complete with pouting mouth.

TOMOAKI SHIMIZU, 1995

ELONGATED CLEATS
on this silver kid Gaultier
ankle boot are the reason
it was once described as a
Transylvanian golf shoe.

JEAN-PAUL GAULTIER, 1993

GAZA BOWEN, 1986

A FEMINIST commentary on the traditional female role, Bowen's "Shoes for the Little Woman" (facing page) were fashioned from scouring pads, sponges and toilet-bowl brushes. "Baby Needs a New Pair of Shoes" is from a series of wearable shoes built with dice and other found objects.

GAZA BOWEN, 1983

A SHOE WITH LEGS is a witty visual conceit, but Bonnaire meant his prototype to immortalize the elegantly long-legged giraffe—an endangered species. The familiar patchwork design was reproduced on calfskin, colored and patterned by hand.

STÉPHANE COUVÉ BONNAIRE,
1996

SAUCY, SILLY and slyly seductive, Cadabra's patent-leather "Maid Shoe" is a female's view of a male sexual fantasy. The plump, curvaceous legs forming the heel nestle beneath a scalloped flounce of white bow, while the maid's "apron" protects the toe.

THEA CADABRA, 1980

PHOTOGRAPHY CREDITS

Every effort has been made to locate all rights holders. If any required acknowledgments or rights have been overlooked, the Publisher will be pleased to rectify any omission in future editions.

Archive Photos: 374 (right, photo by David Lees); Jim Arndt Photography: 328 (right); Courtesy of Joseph Azagury: 34, 43; Bally Shoe Museum: 14 (top left), 15 (bottom right), 132 (top right), 185 (top left), 198 (both), 199, 235, 286 (top), 294, 295 (right), 308, 317, 348 (left), 368, 383, 420 (both), 432; Courtesy of Bally Shoes: 316; Courtesy of The Bata Shoe Museum: 1, 8 (top right), 9 (bottom left), 10 (bottom right), 14 (bottom right), 22 (bottom left), 23, 25 (top left), 26, 28, 29 (both), 30, 32, 36, 37, 40, 41, 45 (both), 59, 78, 79, 80, 81, 82 (Hal Roth Photo), 83, 119, 132 (left), 133, 136, 138, 139, 140, 141, 142, 144, 150, 151, 153, 160 (Hal Roth Photo), 162, 164, 174, 190, 192, 193 (both), 229 (left, on loan from Bally Shoe Museum), 244 (both), 245, 278, 279, 293, 298, 301, 302, 303, 304 (left), 305 (both), 309 (right), 311, 318, 335, 338, 343, 345, 352, 354, 356, 357, 360, 364, 367 (on loan from Bally Shoe Museum), 370, 373, 380, 406, 434, 438 (both), 449, 456, 476 (left), 481, 491; Bavarian National Museum, Munich: 361; Courtesy of Belgian Shoes: 272, 273; Courtesy of Benneton: 230 (right); The Bettmann Archive: 22 (top right), 47 (left), 187, 339 (left); Courtesy of Birkenstock: 290 (both); Courtesy of Manolo Blahnik: 156 (left); Brian Hillier Photography: 76, 248 (shoes from the collection of The Bata Shoe Museum); Courtesy of the Brown Group, Inc.: 243 (left); Courtesy of Centurian Spartacus Publishing Co.: 170 (top right); Courtesy of Chanel: 186 (left), 241, 259, 271, 346, 425; Charles Jourdan Museum: 21, 46 (top right), 47 (bottom right), 48 (top left), 49 (all), 113, 217, 358,

(both), 402, 408, 414, 416, 436, 437, 480; Courtesy of Musei Civici, Venice: 348 (right); Collection, The Museum at The Fashion Institute of Technology: 287; Courtesy of Nike, Inc.: 250; Northampton Museums and Art Gallery: 74, 87, 403, 413, 418 (both), 424, 501; Collection, Norton Family Foundation, Los Angeles, California: 498 (photo by Michael Kirkpatrick); Courtesy of Michel Perry: 404; Courtesy of Andrea Pfister: 16 (bottom right), 57, 69, 118, 155, 175, 484; Rapid Eye © The Conde Nast PL-British *Vogue:* 263 (left), 265 (left); Courtesy of Reebok: 251; © Al Rendon: 331 (both); Courtesy of Rios of Mercedes: 333; Frank Rispoli: 64 (top left), 442; From the collection of Glenn Roberts photos by Ed Pfizenmaier: 152, 312 (both), 313, 401, 405 (left), 444, 445, 448, 450, 451; From the collection of Glenn Roberts, photos © Sheilah Scully: 381, 446, 447; Salvatore Ferragamo Museum: 10 (top left), 51, 62, 63, 120 (left), 218, 355, 374 (left), 375, 376 (both), 433, 459; Cultural History Collection, National Museum of American History, Smithsonian Institution: 462; Courtesy of the Sterling Last Company: 19; © Inez van Lamsweerde: 72; © Inez van Lamsweerde-Vinoodh Matadin: 425 (left); Courtesy of Vivienne Westwood: 427 (right), 428 (left), 429 (left); Courtesy of Jasmin Zorlu: 236.

Cover: (Front) United Nude; (Spine, p. 490) Marina Dempster; (Back cover, left) photo by Ungala; (Back cover, right) photo by Joost van Manen/Jan Jansen

ABOUT THE AUTHOR

Noted design editor and writer Linda O'Keeffe
has been involved in design for over three
decades, including sixteen years as the creative
director at *Metropolitan Home* magazine. She
currently contributes to a variety of shelter and
architecture publications, lectures, moderates
panels, and appears regularly on radio and television design programs. She is also the author of
Brilliant: White in Design and *Stripes: Design
Between The Lines.*